The Federal Aviation Administration

PRAEGER LIBRARY OF U.S. GOVERNMENT DEPARTMENTS
AND AGENCIES

Consulting Editors

ERNEST S. GRIFFITH

Former University Professor and Dean Emeritus, School of International Service, American University; former Director, Legislative Reference Service, Library of Congress; and author of *The American System of Government* and *The Modern Government in Action*

HUGH LANGDON ELSBREE

Former Chairman, Department of Political Science, Dartmouth College; former Managing Editor, *American Political Science Review;* former Director, Legislative Reference Service, Library of Congress

The Federal Aviation Administration

Robert Burkhardt

FREDERICK A. PRAEGER, *Publishers*
New York • Washington • London

FREDERICK A. PRAEGER, PUBLISHERS
111 Fourth Avenue, New York, N.Y. 10003, U.S.A.
77–79 Charlotte Street, London W.1, England

Published in the United States of America in 1967
by Frederick A. Praeger, Inc., Publishers

© 1967 by Robert Burkhardt

Library of Congress Catalog Card Number: 67-24672

Printed in the United States of America

To the FAA's 12,000 air traffic controllers

Preface

Early in 1966, not too long after I began working on this book, President Johnson asked Congress to establish the Department of Transportation. With surprisingly little opposition, at least from the aviation community, Congress was able to hold hearings, mark up a bill, and obtain passage of this major piece of legislation, all within the time span of a few months. As part of the Transportation Act of 1966, the Federal Aviation Agency (FAA) was changed from an independent agency, whose head reported directly to the President, to a subordinate part of the new department.

Except for a name change to the Federal Aviation Administration—which enabled the agency to keep its FAA acronym—there were few outward signs to show that the FAA had lost its independent status, or that its administrator had been downgraded one notch in the official hierarchy. It was the intent of Congress that the FAA be transferred intact into the new department, and there was good reason for doing it this way. Like the Civil Aeronautics Administration, which preceded the FAA, the organization is established around the functions. This means that unless there are unforeseen changes in functions, the FAA is almost certain to continue to do its work in the same way it has in the past.

It has been my good fortune to have been assigned during the past ten years to report both the establishment of the Federal Aviation Agency in 1957 and the coming into existence of the Department of Transportation. Much of the material that follows is taken from my own contemporaneous notes and from the articles and news reports that I wrote at the time. Other material has been supplied by the FAA itself, as well as by officials of the agency, present and former. However, the opinions expressed in this book are my own, and I alone am responsible for them.

ROBERT BURKHARDT

Washington, D.C.

Contents

CHART

A section of photographs follows page 86.

The Federal Aviation Administration

I

Before There Was an FAA

Before there was a Federal Aviation Administration, there was a Federal Aviation Agency, and before there was a Federal Aviation Agency, there was a Civil Aeronautics Administration—and before that a Civil Aeronautics Authority, and before that a Bureau of Air Commerce, and before that there was an Aeronautics Branch in the Department of Commerce.

Of course, before any of these, there were those magnificent Wright brothers, who started the whole thing on a sandy knoll not far from Kitty Hawk, North Carolina, on December 17, 1903.

Today, the Federal Aviation Administration (FAA) is one of the six operating units within the U.S. Department of Transportation. In addition to the FAA, the department is made up of the U.S. Coast Guard, the Federal Highway Administration, the Federal Railroad Administration, and the Saint Lawrence Seaway Development Corporation. An independent National Transportation Safety Board also operates within the department. Of these operating units, the Federal Aviation Administration is the largest, and its basic function is air safety.

THE EARLY YEARS

The Wright brothers were not only the inventors of the airplane—and for a brief period the only commercial aircraft manufacturers in the world—they were also the only air traffic controllers, the only flight safety standards inspectors, and the only flight instructors. When you bought an airplane built by the Wright brothers, you were taught to fly by them and you were given a slip of paper attesting to this fact. These were the first pilot licenses.

It was not until World War I that either pilots or airplanes were turned out in quantity. Under the forced demands of World War I, not only aircraft but pilots were produced in such numbers as to permit standardization of the product for the first time. One result was that both pilots and airplanes emerged from World War I in a state of development which made possible the beginning of practical commercial air transport operations. Even before the war ended, the U.S. government established a regular airmail service between New York and Washington, D.C. The route was first flown by army pilots on May 15, 1918. Civilian pilots were later substituted by the Post Office Department and the U.S. airmail service expanded rapidly. By September, 1920, a transcontinental air route was operating. Because only primitive visual navigation aids were available, the route could be flown only during daylight hours. It was not until 1923 that lighted airway beacons were first installed, along the air route between Chicago and Cheyenne. In those days, it was possible for flights to leave New York westbound, or from San Francisco eastbound, on the morning of one day and reach the opposite coast by the evening of the next day. These transcontinental flights were started on a regular basis in 1924. Regular overnight airmail service between New York and Chicago began in July, 1925. In view of this country's many "firsts" since that time, it is interesting to note that in

1925 the United States was several years behind European countries, which had moved more quickly after the war to establish civil aviation on a commercial basis.

It was not until 1925, when Congress passed the Kelly Airmail Act, that the Post Office withdrew from the flying business and gave the job of carrying the mail to private transport companies. While commercial air transportation was developing its first regular service after World War I under the impact of the Post Office's airmail requirements, private flying—mostly of the barnstorming variety, done by World War I pilots in surplus World War I aircraft—was making a small beginning also. The economics of barnstorming were simple. Anybody with an airplane that had two seats could go into the business. All that was needed was a cow pasture near a town and a small advertisement in the local weekly saying that aerial sightseeing flights would be given for two dollars to all comers.

Where were the government aviation regulators? Many were not even born yet. There was no need for a pilot's license, nor for an airplane airworthiness certificate, and it was a long time before the U.S. government elected to take over the job of regulating and promoting civil aviation. As early as March, 1912, the Aero Club of America in its publication, *Aeronautics,* emphasized the importance of federal registration of aircraft and the licensing of airmen. The Aero Club's idea did not take hold, however, and the club itself issued the first pilot licenses and continued to do so, under the authority of its international charter, until 1926, when Congress passed the Air Commerce Act.

While Congress was reluctant to take over regulation and promotion of the nation's infant commercial aviation efforts, it did realize that future aeronautical progress depended on federal help and guidance. Thus the National Advisory Committee for Aeronautics (NACA) had been created by Congress in 1915 "to supervise and direct the scientific study of the problems of aerial flight, with a view to their practical solution." One of the first things NACA did was press for federal regulation of aeronautics. In 1919, President Wilson submitted to Congress a bill, drafted by NACA, which would authorize the Department of Commerce to license pilots, inspect aircraft, and supervise the use of airfields. No action was taken on President Wilson's recommendation, but bills to regulate this infant industry continued to be introduced one after another until finally, seven years later, in 1926, the Air Commerce Act was passed.

Why was Congress slow to move toward regulation of commercial aviation? One reason was that military aviation was an exciting subject in those days. By 1925, the controversy swirling around the colorful General Billy Mitchell had become so heated that the Acting Secretary of War and the Secretary of the Navy jointly petitioned President Coolidge to appoint a special board to study the subject of aviation. President Coolidge did so, appointing Dwight W. Morrow as chairman. After taking much testimony and hearing from all interested parties, the Morrow Board recommended the separation of military and civil aviation, and the creation of three additional Assistant Secretaries of War, Navy, and Commerce. Each Assistant Secretary should be charged with supervising government aeronautical activities in his special area—military, naval, or civil.

The Air Commerce Act of 1926 was the result of the Morrow Board's recommendations. The same year, Congress set up the posts of Assistant Secretary of War, and Assistant Secretary of the Navy for Aeronautics. On May 20, 1926, President Coolidge signed the Air Commerce Act into law. The act instructed the Secretary of Commerce to do almost all the things being done today by the Federal Aviation Administration: to foster air commerce; designate and establish federal airways; establish, operate, and maintain aids for air navigation (except airports); arrange for research and development to improve such aids; license pilots and other airmen; issue airworthiness certificates for aircraft and major aircraft components; and investigate accidents.

This act has been called the legislative cornerstone for the development of commercial aviation in America. One interesting feature of the 1926 congressional program was a joint resolution, passed on July 3, authorizing the President to detail officers of the Army Air Corps to duty with the Commerce Department in connection with the work of promoting civil aviation. Such detail was to be limited to periods of not more than one year. Herbert Hoover was Secretary of Commerce in 1926, and it was his belief that the duties imposed by the Air Commerce Act should be carried out insofar as possible by the existing organization of his department. As a result, only two new divisions were set up, although the Aeronautics Branch, as it was called, was given authority to direct the work of three other units in the Commerce Department. The two new units were the Air Regulations Division and Air Information Division. The Bureau of Lighthouses was ordered to establish an airways division; the Bureau of Standards was instructed to set up an aeronautical research division; and the Coast and Geodetic Survey was required to have an air-mapping section—which it has to this day. These three existing units received direction from the Aeronautics Branch concerning the work they were to undertake, but they remained administratively outside the framework of the branch.

On August 11, 1926, the President appointed William P. MacCracken, Jr., to be the first Assistant Secretary of Commerce for Aeronautics. MacCracken was a World War I army pilot, former chairman of the American Bar Association Committee on Aviation Law, and an officer of National Air Transport, one of the first airlines, which was organized in 1925 to bid on airmail contracts.

In view of the criticism which is voiced from time to time

over the use of military men in the FAA, it is of interest to note that Secretary Hoover on November 16, 1926, asked the Medical Corps of the Department of the Army to release Dr. Louis H. Bauer to become the first medical director of the Aeronautics Branch. Dr. Bauer was a veteran of thirteen years service in the army, about half of which was with the Air Service.

THE AERONAUTICS BRANCH, 1926–34

To get the Aeronautics Branch off the ground in 1927, Congress appropriated an initial $550,000. This was increased in fiscal 1928 to $3.8 million, and in fiscal 1929 to $5.6 million. In fiscal 1930, even though the depression was forcing widespread government economies, a small increase to $6.7 million was voted. By fiscal 1931, the budget was up to $9.2 million, and the fiscal 1932 budget topped $10 million for the first time. But by fiscal 1933, the depression caught up with the Aeronautics Branch and its budget was cut to $8.6 million. The low point was reached in fiscal 1935, when it had to make do with $5.7 million.

The first of the Aeronautics Branch's regulations required all aircraft, whether used in commercial aeronautics or in private flying, to be registered with the federal government and marked with an assigned identification number. All pilots engaged in interstate commerce were required to obtain either transport or industrial pilot licenses, or both. Mechanics were required to obtain either engine or airframe mechanic licenses, or both. Air traffic rules were issued at the same time, generally based on highway and maritime rules.

In March, 1927, the first certificate of aircraft type was issued to a three-place, 200-horsepower, open biplane called the Buhl Airster. Two months later, on May 20–21, a young airmail pilot, Charles A. Lindbergh, made the first nonstop solo flight across the Atlantic Ocean in a heavier-than-air craft—the "Spirit of St. Louis." His elapsed time was 33 hours, 29 minutes, and 30 seconds, for a distance of 3,610 miles. In June of the same year, control of the Transcontinental Airways System was transferred from the Post Office Department to the Department of Commerce. This was an airway extending from New York to San Francisco, for a distance of 2,612 miles, about 600 miles of which were not lighted by beacons. Its air navigation facilities included 92 intermediate airfields, 101 electric beacons, 417 acetylene beacons, and 17 radio stations, manned by 45 radio operators, 14 maintenance mechanics, and 84 caretakers.

That same summer, the Aeronautics Branch offered for sale the first airway strip map, covering a route from Moline, Illinois, to Kansas City, Missouri. And during this momentous year Pan American Airways began the first scheduled international commercial flight service between Key West, Florida, and Havana, Cuba. In the fall of 1927, the fourth International Air Congress, held in Rome, dealt mainly with civil aviation affairs, including such subjects as promotion of civil aeronautics, regulations required for international flights, high-altitude flying, and judicial and legal matters of an international air commerce nature. At the end of this historic year, a conference was held by the Secretary of Commerce with Lindbergh and the fourteen other fliers that had made transocean crossings during the year. One of the practical purposes of the conference was to get the pilot viewpoint on meteorological conditions and weather forecasting needs.

On June 15, 1933, shortly after President Franklin Roosevelt was sworn into office, the position of director of Aeronautics was established within the Commerce Department to take the place of the Assistant Secretary for Aeronautics. Under the reorganization that followed, two assistant directorships were established—for air regulation and air navigation. In October, Eugene L. Vidal was appointed director of the Aeronautics Branch. One of Mr. Vidal's first acts was to persuade the Public Works Administration to make $500,000 available for such research and development as might be necessary to produce a low-cost airplane. He also established an "amateur grade" rating for pilots who had twenty-five hours of solo flying time.

Those in the Department of Commerce who were responsible for civil aviation affairs worked quietly and without fanfare. As a result, they were for the most part untouched either by the heated controversy over the place of aviation in military affairs, or by the airmail scandals of 1933 and 1934. Acting on persistent reports of irregularities in the awarding of airmail contracts, a Senate investigating committee, chaired by Senator Hugo L. Black of Alabama, confirmed investigations made by the Post Office Department that revealed that competitive bidding for flying the mail had been by-passed, and contract awards had been made as the result of collusion. These findings prompted President Roosevelt to order the cancellation of all existing mail contracts, effective at midnight, February 19, 1934. At the same time, the President directed the Secretary of War to make available such planes and pilots as were necessary to carry the airmail during the crisis. In only a few weeks, however, crashes had taken the lives of ten army flyers—four while flying the mail routes and six in related flying. On March 10, President Roosevelt ordered a temporary curtailment of airmail service by the Army Air Corps. Nine days later, the army resumed carrying the mail and continued its schedules until May 8, 1934, at which time service by commercial companies began again on some of the routes. The Air Corps' last scheduled flight was June 1, 1934.

Some of the disclosures in the airmail scandal prompted Senator Patrick McCarran of Nevada to introduce a bill in March, 1934, that would provide for the creation of a federal aviation commission to carry out the economic regulation of scheduled air carrier operations. This was the first of a series of bills which Senator McCarran introduced in an effort to create an independent aviation regulatory agency. His efforts, along with those of Representative Clarence Lea and others, finally resulted in passage of the Civil Aeronautics Act of 1938.

Because of the inadequacy of the Army Air Corps, as revealed by the poor showing made in carrying the mail during the emergency, the Secretary of War appointed a committee to report on the efficiency of its technical flying equipment and training. The committee was composed of former Secretary of War Newton D. Baker, chairman, five other civilians, and five military members.

THE BUREAU OF AIR COMMERCE, 1934–38

In July, 1934—the same month that the name of the Aeronautics Branch was changed to the Bureau of Air Commerce by order of the Secretary of Commerce—the Baker committee issued its report. It had heard testimony from 105 witnesses, had visited various aviation centers, and had received 536 communications from Air Corps officers. According to the report, the United States was ahead of other countries in general, commercial, and naval aviation, but military aviation needed more financial support. Practically all the deficiencies in the Air Corps were traceable to lack of funds. Since aviation industry was essential to national defense, the committee recommended that the government stop all activities that were competitive with the private aviation effort and that the Army Air Corps take steps to keep up with the latest commercial equipment and methods. The committee also recommended the training of army pilots in the use of the national airway system and the development of army cargo and transport planes.

While this was going on, the Airmail Act of 1934 was passed and signed by the President. One of its provisions authorized the President to appoint a commission of five members "for the purpose of making an immediate study and survey and to report to Congress not later than February 1, 1935, its recommendations of a broad policy covering all phases of aviation and the relation of the United States thereto." President Roosevelt lost no time in appointing the Federal Aviation Commission, with Clarke Howell, editor of *The Atlanta Constitution,* as chairman. The commission, in its report, recommended that aviation be placed on the same regulatory basis as land transportation. To fix airmail rates and to carry out other economic regulations of the industry, Congress should create a temporary, independent air commerce commission to promote sound competitive practices and to discourage holding company operations and other devices which would lead to monopoly. The Post Office Department should no longer be limited to specific contracts, but should be free to use existing route services for the carriage of airmail.

The Federal Aviation Commission further recommended that the safety regulating functions of the Bureau of Air Commerce be transferred to the proposed air commerce commission. The Bureau of Air Commerce's remaining functions were to be allowed to be continued without change except for airports. Since it was necessary to encourage expansion of airports through the installation of lights and other navigational aids, the federal government should share maintenance costs with the local agencies when the airport was designated by the air commerce commission as essential to interstate commerce. The commission's report did not favor direct government ownership of commercial aviation companies, even though this was the almost universal situation in Europe. Competition was to be the keynote and airline operators were not to have a monopoly on the routes they served.

As a result of cutthroat competitive bidding under the Airmail Act, which permitted the Postmaster General to contract with private flyers to carry the mail, the industry was in a precarious position. The Federal Aviation Commission found commercial air services generally being operated at a loss, which contributed to aviation's poor safety record. To correct the problem, at least in part, it was recommended that the government subsidize the carriers in the form of extra mail pay. As part of the public subsidy benefits, and to insure the orderly development of the infant industry, the airlines should also be regulated as a public utility, and fares and rates should be controlled by the federal government. This would further assure financial capability and also avoid undue concentration of ownership.

President Roosevelt endorsed some of the recommendations contained in the report of his Federal Aviation Commission, but not the one that called for creation of a temporary air commerce commission. He favored using those administrative agencies that had functioned well in the past rather than creating new ones. The proper agency to serve the economic regulatory needs of air transportation would be a division of the Interstate Commerce Commission.

The President's views were reflected by Senator McCarran in a new bill, a basic feature of which was the shifting of all regulatory authority to the Interstate Commerce Commission, but the bill died with the adjournment of the Seventy-Fourth Congress in 1936.

In 1938, an Airport Traffic Control Section was created in the Airways Operation Division of the Bureau of Air Commerce to standardize airport control-tower equipment, operational techniques, and personnel training. Within six months, forty airport control operators had been certificated by this new section. Then, early in 1938, President Roosevelt advised Senator McCarran and Congressman Lea that he had changed his mind about making the Interstate Commerce Commission responsible for air commerce regulations and now favored the idea of a separate commission to regulate all phases of civil aeronautics. Finally, in June, 1938, the Civil Aeronautics Act was passed by the Congress and signed by President Roosevelt, creating a new kind of independent federal aviation agency, which would keep its functions as an agent of Congress separate from its functions as an agent of the President.

THE CIVIL AERONAUTICS AUTHORITY, 1938–40

To perform the functions of safety and economic regulation of civil aeronautics, the law created a five-member Civil Aeronautics Authority (not to be confused with the Civil Aeronautics Administration, which did not see the light of day until 1940). In addition, it created the office of Civil Aeronautics administrator, which would operate within the Authority and be responsible for the executive and operational functions of the new agency. Also created within the Civil Aeronautics Authority was an Air Safety Board, made up of three members who were to exercise judicial powers in determining the cause of accidents.

The Air Safety Board was authorized both to investigate accidents and to make recommendations for improved air safety regulations. It operated independently and could not be assigned other types of work. One member of the Air Safety Board was required to have had at least 3,000 hours of flight time in scheduled air transportation. The Air Safety Board was not regulatory in nature; it was intended to be a fact-finding body and an independent investigator of the results of such regulations as the Civil Aeronautics Authority might issue.

The 1938 Act had as its purpose "the encouragement and development of a commercial air transportation system intended to meet the present and future needs of the foreign and domestic commerce of the U.S., of the postal service and of national defense." The highest level of safety was to be maintained. The objective was adequate, efficient, and economic air service at reasonable charges, without discrimination, preference, or advantage to any shipper or traveler, and without unfair or destructive competition.

The regulation of air safety was essentially that which had previously been performed by the Bureau of Air Commerce, with some revision and enlargement. Economic regulations were also made more comprehensive. The Civil Aeronautics Authority was given regulatory powers covering airline tariffs, airmail rates, and the business practices of the airlines, including inspection and regulation of such items as accounts, records, consolidations, mergers, or other forms of control, as well as methods of competition.

The functions of the Civil Aeronautics administrator under the new law were to foster civil aeronautics and commerce, to establish civil airways, to provide for technical improvement of air navigation facilities for the airways, and to protect and regulate air traffic along the airways. The administrator was prohibited from acquiring any airport either by purchase or condemnation, but he was allowed to provide technical improvements for airports owned by public authorities.

President Roosevelt named Edward J. Noble of Connecticut chairman of the Civil Aeronautics Authority. Mr. Noble was a businessman and industrialist who had a long-standing interest in aviation and was one of the first private owners of an autogiro. Clinton M. Hester of Montana was appointed as the agency's first administrator. Mr. Hester had served in six federal agencies and was, at the time of his appointment, assistant general counsel of the Treasury Department.*

In 1939, the Civil Aeronautics Authority was given the responsibility under a new law for the training of civilian pilots. The objective was to provide sufficient training to

---

* See Appendix B for a complete list of administrators of the FAA and its predecessor organizations.

prepare a student for a private pilot certificate. A total of $5.6 million was appropriated for the program during fiscal years 1939 and 1940. Then, in June, 1940, President Roosevelt announced a reorganization plan to clarify the relations of the administrator of the Civil Aeronautics Authority to its five-member board. Under the reorganization, the five-man authority was transferred to the Department of Commerce and renamed the Civil Aeronautics Board (CAB). At the same time, the Air Safety Board was abolished and its accident investigating functions were assigned to the new CAB. Though the CAB was to report to Congress as well as to the President through the Secretary of Commerce, it was to exercise its functions of rule-making, adjudication, and investigation independently of the Secretary.

The Civil Aeronautics Administration, 1940–58

The Civil Aeronautics administrator, with the new title of administrator of Civil Aeronautics, was also transferred to the Department of Commerce, where, under the designation Civil Aeronautics Administration, he was to function under the direction and supervision of the Secretary. His jobs were to include the ones initially assigned to him by the Civil Aeronautics Act of 1938, plus certain safety-regulating duties delegated to him as supervisor of the Bureau of Safety Regulations. These safety-regulating duties did not involve rule-making, or the power to suspend or revoke certificates. The Civil Aeronautics Authority continued as a paper organization which embraced both the CAB and the new Civil Aeronautics Administration (CAA), but it performed no function.

Lieutenant Colonel Donald H. Connelly, USA, was confirmed by the Senate as the first administrator of Civil Aeronautics. A graduate of West Point, class of 1910, Colonel Connelly had served in the Corps of Engineers since leaving the military academy. He was director of the Public Works

Administration in Los Angeles in 1934 and administrator of the Works Projects Administration for Southern California from 1935 to 1939.

In October, 1940, Congress appropriated $40 million for construction, improvement, and repair of up to 250 public airports. This was the first appropriation for airport construction made by Congress directly to a federal aviation agency. To qualify for federal funds, a determination had to be made that the improvements were necessary for national defense. Determination of the national defense character of the airports eligible for aid was to be made by the Civil Aeronautics administrator, with the approval of a board composed of the Secretaries of War, Navy, and Commerce. Designation of 193 sites took place promptly after enactment of the law and, to expedite construction, the CAA made cooperative arrangements with the War and Navy Departments and the Works Projects Administration, which undertook actual construction.

In 1940, the CAA commissioned an intercontinental radio station in New York to provide a two-way radio communication with aircraft operating across the Atlantic. In January of the following year, the CAA established a standardization center at Houston, Texas. The purpose of the center was to get as much uniformity as possible in the CAA's inspection and instruction methods and in its examinations for all types of airman certificates. All flight and inspection personnel were to take periodic refresher courses at the center, and new CAA employees were to receive a course of instruction there before assignment to their regular post of duty.

During World War II, the Civil Aeronautics Administration remained a part of the Department of Commerce and quietly continued its work of civil air traffic control. Several attempts were made at this time to "coordinate" government aviation affairs, but on the whole these were not very successful.

Then, on March 27, 1945, an interdepartmental memorandum was signed by the Departments of State, War, Navy, and Commerce, setting up an Air Coordinating Committee to integrate and coordinate federal aviation policy. The committee was formally established in September, 1946. It was terminated by Executive Order 10883 in October, 1960, almost entirely on the basis of the recommendation of its last chairman, Lieutenant General Elwood R. Quesada. Quesada believed that the usefulness of the committee was more than outweighed by the fact that reference to the Air Coordinating Committee often meant an end to a project. From long experience in government service, he had come to believe that the way to bring progress to a halt in any area of government activity was to set up a committee. The Air Coordinating Committee had often served as a burial ground for some of the CAA's better ideas. Quesada found fewer and fewer reasons to convene the committee while he was chairman; in the end, he cheerfully presided over its abolition.

Considering the nature of the Air Coordinating Committee, it was not surprising that this interagency group played little or no part in the work that led to the passage of the Federal Aviation Act. One group which helped prepare the way for the FAA was a special aviation study group named by President Harry Truman in July, 1947. The so-called Air Policy Commission was instructed by the President to make an objective inquiry into national aviation policies and problems with an eye to assisting the President in formulating an integrated aviation policy.

At the end of 1947, the commission submitted a report, "Survival in the Air Age," which urged immediate action to strengthen the military air services and also suggested major changes in the organization of the CAA. The commission recommended the establishment of an office of civil aviation and an office of industry and trade, both headed by assistant secretaries reporting directly to the Secretary of Commerce.

CAA's functions, plus the Civil Aeronautics Board's responsibility for safety regulations were to be incorporated into a new department of civil aviation. It was also suggested that CAB's responsibility be limited to rate and route decisions and that an Air Safety Board be established with the responsibility for investigating aviation accidents.

II

Federal Aviation Comes of Age

On January 20, 1953, Dwight D. Eisenhower, the only President ever to have held a private pilot's license, was inaugurated. In May, 1955, at the request of President Eisenhower, the director of the Bureau of the Budget asked William Barclay Harding, a Wall Street investment broker with considerable aviation experience, to serve as a consultant and to develop recommendations on the following questions: (1) Should a study of long-range needs for aviation facilities and aids be undertaken? (2) What should be the coverage of such a study, if it should be made, including an indication of specific areas and subjects which seem to require particular attention? (3) How could such a study, if made, best be organized and conducted?

To assist Mr. Harding, the President appointed six prominent aviation leaders. This aviation facilities study group submitted its report to the director of the Bureau of the Budget in December, 1955. The need to improve air traffic management had reached a critical point and it was recommended that an individual of national reputation, responsible directly to the President, be appointed to provide full-time, high level leadership in developing a program for solving the complex technical and organizational problems facing the government and the aviation industry.

In line with the Harding committee recommendations,

President Eisenhower in February, 1956, appointed Edward P. Curtis as his special assistant for aviation facilities planning. Mr. Curtis's assignment was to direct and coordinate a long-range study of the nation's aviation requirements. He was also to develop a comprehensive plan for meeting, in the most effective and economical manner, the needs disclosed by his study, and to formulate legislative, organizational, administrative, and budgetary recommendations to carry out the plan.

THE FEDERAL AVIATION ACT

In May, 1957, Edward Curtis submitted his report on aviation facilities planning. This report warned of "a crisis in the making" as a result of the inability of the CAA's airspace management system to cope with the complex problems of both civil and military traffic. The growing congestion of airspace was inhibiting military flying and retarding the progress of air commerce. Many excellent plans for improving the nation's aviation facilities had failed to come to fruition in the past because of the inability of the government to keep up with aviation's dynamic growth. To correct this, the report recommended the establishment of an independent federal aviation agency, in which would be consolidated all the essential management functions necessary to support the common needs of U.S. military and civilian aviation. Until such a permanent agency could be created, it was proposed that an airways modernization board be set up as an independent agency, responsible for developing and consolidating requirements for future systems of communications, navigation, and air traffic control.

In July, 1957, President Eisenhower appointed General Elwood R. Quesada as his special assistant for aviation affairs, and directed him to secure the implementation of the Curtis plan of action.

Acting with unusual speed, Congress approved the Airways Modernization Act (Public Law 85-133), establishing an Airways Modernization Board "to provide for the development and modernization of the national system of navigation and traffic control facilities to serve present and future needs of civil and military aviation." The Act provided for a temporary three-member board—consisting of a chairman, appointed by the President, and representatives of the Secretaries of Defense and Commerce—to be terminated on June 30, 1960. General Quesada was nominated by the President as chairman of the board and was confirmed by the Senate on August 16, 1957.

On June 13, 1958, President Eisenhower, in his message to Congress, recommended the prompt enactment of legislation to establish an independent federal aviation agency. Most of the work done by Congress in drafting the Federal Aviation Act was done by the Senate Commerce Committee —in particular, by the Aviation Subcommittee, chaired by Senator A. S. Mike Monroney of Oklahoma. The urgent need for legislation was made evident by two midair collisions early in 1958. Both crashes were caused, at least in part, by the fact that two different air traffic control systems, one military and the other civilian, were allocating the same airspace. Leaders in the Senate and the House put their weight behind the bill; after some initial hesitation, mostly from the Bureau of the Budget, which would have preferred a department of transportation, the White House also gave its full support. The Bureau of the Budget was able to generate little support outside of the government for the idea of a separate transportation agency.

The Defense Department had an active and efficient air traffic control system under its jurisdiction and was very reluctant to turn its system loose without some guarantee that in time of war it would get it back. General Quesada's statement to Congress in support of the Federal Aviation

Act contained assurances to the military that their views and interests would be treated with great consideration. He set forth five requirements that had to be met by the new agency:

1. *Allocation and use of airspace.* The new agency must have "full and paramount" authority over allocation and use of airspace by both civil and military aircrafts.

2. *Recognition of military needs.* In the control of airspace by the new agency, recognition must be given to national defense interests. "All of us recognize that our military structure must permit a quick response to acts of aggression."

3. *Need for military participation.* Successful consolidation of the essential airspace management functions common to civil and military aviation require active participation by military personnel in the activities of the new agency.

4. *Consolidation of safety rule-making.* A single authority to develop safety regulations is essential in order to eliminate loss of time, duplication of effort, and management confusion.

5. *Support for military operations.* This agency will administer functions in direct support of military air operations. "It is essential, therefore, that legislation be developed to assure the stability and continued service of essential personnel in a military emergency."

General Quesada noted that the responsibility for allocating airspace was presently divided: "Under the provisions of the Civil Aeronautics Act, the Civil Aeronautics Board is authorized to delegate its authority, or portions thereof, to the Civil Aeronautics Administration, and as a matter of practice, it does so in large measure. . . . It is of utmost importance that the final administrative say on these rules be lodged in an agency of the executive branch, directly responsible for resolving the needs of all users—civil and military."

Emphasizing the military role in airspace use, General Quesada, drawing on his experience as a wartime Air Force commander, claimed that the air had become a major battleground for the conduct of both offensive and defensive warfare.

It is necessary, therefore, that there be built into the airspace control mechanism a recognition of imperative military necessity in an emergency. The compression of time in a military emergency will not permit debate or negotiations for airspace assignment to hamper military operations in defense of our country. Provision must be made for military departure from peacetime procedures when emergency arises or urgent military necessity requires decisive action. The nation cannot afford to inhibit essential military operations which may have to be triggered with little notice. At the same time, the military in exercising its authority in the public interest must give the earliest practicable prior notice of its intentions to the new agency.

General Quesada was equally emphatic in explaining the need for military participation in the new agency. He felt that the use of military personnel in merely advisory positions would not be enough; the agency would need military participation—not representation.

Because of a latent, but very real, concern by the civilian users of the airspace that the military meant to get their foot in the door and take over the agency if they could, it was decided by both administration and congressional leaders not to attempt to solve this military participation problem within the framework of the new law. Such an effort, it was believed, would result in no law at all; the best solution would be to take up the problem in later amendments to the law, which could be debated separately.

General Quesada expressed the administration's view on this segmented approach to the Federal Aviation Act: "The solution to this problem is complicated and will require additional legislation, which will be proposed to the Congress at an early date. In the meantime, provisions should remain in the bill giving the President interim authority to transfer the agency intact into the Department of Defense." As it turned out, such authority was never included in the bill, and efforts to get Congress to give reserve military status to key air traffic control personnel were never successful.

On the purely administrative side, General Quesada addressed himself to the need for consolidating the making of safety rules. Under the Civil Aeronautics Act, responsibility for issuing and administering safety regulations was divided between two government agencies—the Civil Aeronautics Board and the Civil Aeronautics Administration. The CAB was primarily concerned with the regulation and promotion of air commerce, but it also issued and amended the Civil Air Regulations. The CAA, which was primarily concerned with operating the nation's airways, was also called on to administer the CAB's regulations. This division of responsibility, according to Quesada, was neither practical nor effective. The drafters of the new legislation wisely proposed changing this arrangement by placing in the new agency the combined responsibility for both creating and administrating air traffic control systems, for developing the operating rules based on experience and technical understanding, and also for administrating them.*

On August 23, 1958, the President signed into law the Federal Aviation Act, repealing the Air Commerce Act of 1926, the Civil Aeronautics Act of 1938, the Airways Modernization Act of 1957, and those portions of the various Presidential reorganization plans that dealt with civil aviation. The act assigned the functions exercised under these repealed laws to two independent agencies—the Federal Aviation Agency, newly created by the Act, and the Civil Aeronautics Board, whose previous administrative ties to the

* For a complete report on how the final legislation was drafted, see Emmette S. Redford, *Congress Passes the Federal Aviation Act of 1958* (University, Ala.: University of Alabama Press, 1961), Case Study 62. For a shorter report, see "The Inside Story of the Aviation Act," *American Aviation*, June 16, 1958.

Department of Commerce were at last severed. CAB retained responsibility for economic regulations of air carriers as well as for accident investigation, but lost most of its authority in the area of safety regulations and enforcement. This authority was absorbed by the FAA, but the law provided that any FAA order involving suspension or revocation of a certificate might be appealed to the CAB for a *de novo* hearing, after which the CAB had the authority to affirm, amend, modify, or reverse the FAA administrator. Provision was made for FAA participation in accident investigation, but determination of probable cause was reserved to the CAB alone.

Nucleus of the new agency was the Civil Aeronautics Administration, but the FAA also took over responsibilities and personnel of the Airways Modernization Board and the Air Coordinating Committee, whose functions were transferred to the FAA for purposes of liquidation.

Section 103 of the Federal Aviation Act summarizes the basic responsibilities of the FAA administrator:

1. The regulation of air commerce in such manner as to best promote its development and safety and fulfill the requirements of national defense;

2. The promotion, encouragement, and development of civil aeronautics;

3. The control of the use of navigable airspace of the United States and the regulation of both civil and military operations in such airspace in the interest of the safety and efficiency of both;

4. The consolidation of research and development with respect to air navigation facilities, as well as the installation and operation thereof;

5. The development and operation of a common system of air traffic control and navigation for both military and civil aircraft.

These five responsibilities were taken in large measure from the declaration of policy in the Civil Aeronautics Act of 1938. Under the new 1958 Act, the Civil Aeronautics Board was assigned some tasks that duplicated those of the FAA, namely, the encouragement, development, and regulation of air transportation, the promotion of adequate, economical, and efficient service by air carriers, and the regulation of air commerce in such a manner as best to promote air safety.

It is perhaps significant, at least for general aviation, that in Section 104 of the 1958 Act the right of transit in U.S. airspace is broadened. This was done by changing the sentence in Section 3 that began: "There is hereby recognized and declared to exist on behalf of any citizen of the United States a public right of freedom of transit in air commerce through the navigable airspace of the United States." The words "in air commerce" were struck out of the Civil Aeronautics Act, thus giving private flyers equal right to the use of the airspace for their personal, as well as business, flying.

The 1958 report of the Conference Committee is an indication, perhaps, of the seriousness with which these relatively minor word changes were viewed. This committee was given the job of settling differences between the House and Senate versions of the Federal Aviation Act. The report noted, by way of explaining changes, that Section 2 of the Civil Aeronautics Act stated, in effect, that one of the objectives of that Act was "the encouragement and development of Civil Aeronautics." This clause has been carried over into the declarations of policy agreed to in the conference but, said the Conference Committee, "the word 'promotion' has been inserted before the word 'encouragement.' "

The committee went on to say that some fear had been expressed, in the case of the declaration of policy applicable to the CAB, that the addition of this word might be regarded as evidence that Congress wished the board to change in some way the economic regulatory policies or interpretations developed during the past twenty years under the existing law. The addition of this word, however, was not intended to have any such effect.

Exactly what change was intended by the addition of the word "promotion" is not made clear. In general, both the Civil Aeronautics Board and the FAA administrator have treated these vague declarations of policy as they pleased. In reviewing actions of the two agencies, the courts have generally paid more attention to the specific powers delegated to the agencies by the Act than to the general policy statements made either in the Act itself or in the reports which accompanied the Act at the time of passage.

THE NEW AGENCY

When the Federal Aviation Agency was created in 1958, it was intended to be more than just an independent Civil Aeronautics Administration, or an enlarged Airways Modernization Board, or a revamped civil-military and civil air communications service, although it incorporated the responsibilities and, in many cases, the entire staffs of these predecessor organizations. During its last year as an independent agency, the FAA was the eighth largest agency in the federal government, with a staff of more than 43,000 and an annual budget of nearly three-quarters of a billion dollars— a billion, if funds for the supersonic transport project are included.

One reason the FAA, as an agency, turned out to be greater than the sum of its parts has been the strong personalities of the men selected by the President to be FAA administrators. Two have been highly successful Air Force generals; the third was a colorful lawyer and test pilot. The stories of these three men will be told in detail in the chapter that follows.

CIVILIAN VERSUS MILITARY CONTROL

For more than a quarter of a century, as we have seen, until the passage of the Federal Aviation Act in 1958, the Department of Commerce was the key agency in matters of U.S. aviation policy. The Civil Aeronautics Administration had grown to the point where it represented more than half of the department, both in terms of the budget and in numbers of persons employed. Secretaries of Commerce had seen their aviation organization grow steadily over the years, more or less in step with the postwar growth of private and commercial flying. Thus it reflects great credit both on the Commerce Department and on Sinclair Weeks, its Secretary, that wholehearted support was given the decision made by President Eisenhower to take away the largest part of this old and respected department and set it up as an independent aviation agency. It may or may not be significant that both Secretary Weeks and his Under Secretary, Louis S. Rothschild, resigned from government only a short time afterward, but, in retrospect, it seems clear that the aviation industry owed Mr. Weeks and Mr. Rothschild a debt of gratitude for their statesmanlike decision to support rather than oppose the idea of an independent FAA.

Defense Department officials, on the other hand, drove a harder bargain in return for their cooperation. When the 1957 Curtis report was circulated to the Department of Defense, the military concurred in the general concept of a jointly staffed federal aviation agency. This concurrence, however, was based on defense participation on a basis of "full partnership," with the post of deputy administrator filled by a military representative. Unless the new agency provided for a full partnership relationship between civil and military interests, defense officials believed they could never be sure defense needs would be given proper recognition.

In return for full partnership, the military, and particularly the Air Force, were prepared to give up a limited amount of their air traffic and airspace control. Military aircraft had always been responsible to military air traffic controllers. Control towers at military airfields were invariably operated by uniformed military personnel. Blocks of airspace were preempted by the military, some permanently and some on a temporary basis, under procedures which gave civilian airspace users little opportunity to protest the exclusive military use of key air route corridors. The military correctly foresaw that creation of a strong and independent Federal Aviation Agency would result not only in a slowing down of their acquisition of existing airspace, but would also result in an actual return to civilian use of large blocks of airspace that were no longer needed. This is exactly what happened. During the first eighteen months of the FAA, thousands of square miles of airspace were removed from military control and returned to either civil or joint use.

The Curtis report had recommended that responsibility for military air traffic control for the continental United States be transferred from the Air Force to the FAA. The Pentagon had been less then enthusiastic, but at first there was no direct opposition. In its official position paper on this subject, the Department of Defense stated: "The consolidation of civil and military air traffic control and safety communications activities into a jointly managed agency appears to have considerable merit." One of the merits was a reduction in the number of military air traffic control personnel. Such a reduction "would go a long way in solving any management problems faced by the military in this field, i.e., short tenure of military personnel, insufficient number of personnel adequately trained in air traffic control to man overseas bases, and inequities of pay." There were also budget advantages in having one air traffic control agency instead of two. Another distinct advantage was that the FAA "would have to adopt a national approach, accommodating both military and civil interest in air traffic control and flight safety." And, if the Federal Aviation Act or some subsequent legislation were to provide for the automatic transfer of civilian air traffic controllers into uniformed military service in time of war, it would, said the Department of Defense, "enable the head of the jointly managed activities within FAA to establish a firm table of organization, fully manned, which could be counted on to provide continuity of operations during any emergency or war."

What did the Department of Defense have in mind? The public record is not too clear, but probably an arrangement was favored similar to the one which makes the Coast Guard a civilian agency in time of peace and a uniformed service in the defense establishment in time of war. At the time the Federal Aviation Act was written, careful consideration was given to the department's need for automatic command over the FAA's air traffic controllers in time of war. After much private debate, the drafting staff, under the direction of Senator A. S. Mike Monroney, decided that this was too controversial a provision to be included in the Act. The feeling of congressional leaders was that so many improvisations and changes were being made in setting up the FAA that it would take every effort on the part of the leaders of both houses to get the bill through Congress intact. In view of the widely held belief that the military were supporting the establishment of the FAA only because they thought this would enable the Air Force to assume greater rather than lesser control over both civil and military air traffic, a provision which automatically transferred the responsibility for all air traffic operations to the military might make it impossible to persuade a doubtful Congress to pass any legislation at all. More than one attempt has been made since 1958 to add this provision in the form of an amendment, but there is no congressional enthusiasm even now for giving the military any more control in time of war then is absolutely necessary.

APPOINTMENT OF THE FIRST ADMINISTRATOR

There are some who feel that, while the military may have lost this battle, they achieved their goal through domination of the top job in the agency. In spite of the congressional intent clearly expressed in the Federal Aviation Act to have the job of administrator filled by a civilian, two of the first three administrators of the agency were retired Air Force generals. Only during the tenure of the second administrator, Najeeb E. Halaby, was the proper balance of a civilian chief and a military deputy maintained.

President Eisenhower was not in sympathy with the idea that restrictions should be placed on the appointment of military officers to top jobs in the FAA. His principal aviation adviser, Elwood R. Quesada, was a colorful and personable lieutenant general on the retired list of the regular Air Force, with twenty-seven years of active service before retiring in 1951. As the principal architect of the new Federal Aviation Agency, General Quesada was generous enough not to read anything personal into the congressional feeling that a military officer should never be head of the agency. At the same time, he was not averse to becoming the first FAA administrator and was prepared to make whatever sacrifices might be necessary to qualify for the post. A man of independent means, Quesada had devoted himself to private business interests until appointed special White House assistant for aviation matters in 1957. A series of moves by the White House in the fall of 1958 prepared the way for the general to take over as FAA administrator. President Eisenhower announced his intention to appoint General Quesada on September 30, 1958, in a statement, which explained that Quesada would resign his commission as a retired Air Force officer, giving up a substantial pension along with the prerogatives of a retired lieutenant general.

President Eisenhower complained of the provision in the Federal Aviation Act which made this necessary: "The fact that a man of Mr. Quesada's qualifications is obliged to resign his retired status in the regular Air Force to comply with the letter of the law so he can again serve his country does not, in my opinion, seem logical or desirable." The President then announced that he would ask Congress when it convened in January to adopt legislation to except General Quesada from the civilian-only requirement of the Act.

Legislation was passed enabling General Quesada automatically to resume his previous retired rank following his tour of duty as FAA administrator. Before this was done, General Quesada, to comply with the law, resigned his commission as a retired Air Force officer. This cleared the way for the Senate to confirm him as the first FAA administrator, which it did, but not without a fight. The most articulate spokesman in the anti-military group was the late Clair Engle, Democratic Senator from California, whose promising political career was cut short by his untimely death of cancer. A private pilot himself, Senator Engle was a tough, outspoken friend of the "little guy" in aviation—the private and business pilot who had neither time nor money to maintain a lobbyist in Washington to speak for him. On March 11, 1959, he told his fellow senators in one of his few speeches on the floor: "It was with some misgivings that I voted, as a member of the Committee on Interstate and Foreign Commerce, for the confirmation of General Quesada as Administrator of the Federal Aviation Agency."

Why the misgivings? Because, said Senator Engle, he had five reservations regarding General Quesada's possible approach to the problems he could expect to face as FAA administrator:

1. He was concerned because General Quesada was a military officer, whereas the law was clear in requiring that the administrator's job be filled by a civilian. It would be only natural for the general to lean heavily on military thinking and the views of his former comrades-in-arms. Not only General Quesada but other military officers would be serving on the FAA staff. Such officers, when they finish their FAA tour of duty, would go back to the service which loaned them, and there they might be judged, perhaps unfairly, on how well they had represented the point of view of their service while they had been with the FAA. Senator Engle said, "The idea that a military officer, beholden to his own service for the future of his career, will argue very strongly on policy matters with the top men in his career service is, to my way of thinking, naïve."

2. Senator Engle feared that General Quesada did not have an impartial attitude toward the various users of the U.S. airspace and, in fact, might be prejudiced against private fliers and other general aviation users of the airways system. (In his confirmation hearing, General Quesada had denied having such a prejudice; Senator Engle took notice of this in his speech.)

3. The Senator was concerned about General Quesada's attitude that hardware and blackboxes (commercially produced electronic components) were the solution to most air safety problems. "Some of us are concerned that the regulations and requirements for equipment will get so heavy that most general aviation will in fact be grounded," Senator Engle said. "Then, along with the rest of the taxpayers, we will pay the cost of high-priced electric gismos and thousands of FAA employees to chaperone the airline and military pilots through thousands of miles of bare airspace."

4. Continued military requisitioning of public airspace was also of concern to Senator Engle. He conceded that restricting areas of airspace to certain types of military flying

was certainly necessary, but that it ought to be considered in connection with other flying requirements, including those of the air carriers and general aviation. He noted that in his own state, California, restricted areas comprised 22 per cent of the airspace south of San Francisco, and that flight test areas encompassed nearly three-quarters of the entire airspace of the state.

5. Finally, Senator Engle was concerned about General Quesada's attitude toward airport construction, particularly the use of federal funds for such purposes. "The airport program should not be cut off just because the commercial carriers have gotten what they need," said the Senator, nor should a top-heavy proportion of funds be allocated to air carrier airports, since public transport airlines use only 560 of the country's more than 7,000 airports. More small civilian airports were needed. The Senator claimed he "would feel a little more comfortable about General Quesada as FAA administrator if we believed that either his background or his viewpoint was more in the direction of continuing to build this necessary link in our transportation system."

As it turned out, none of Senator Engle's reservations about Quesada's appointment was justified. Except for a tendency to be abrupt with his subordinates—who privately complained they found the general hard to talk to on any kind of a give-and-take basis—General Quesada brought very little of what is often thought of as a dictatorial military attitude with him into the FAA job. His long service not only as commanding general, but as a command pilot, did cause him to emphasize the chain-of-command concept of administration a little heavily, but many who watched him closely during his service as FAA administrator felt that the sprawling and sometimes unresponsive FAA staff was the better for a touch of military discipline. Whatever drawbacks he may have inherited from his military career were more than compensated for by his hard-driving attention to detail and his insistence on long-range agency planning. In his bringing together the diverse elements of the CAA, the Airways Modernization Board, and the safety rule making section of the Civil Aeronautics Board, General Quesada did a superior job in setting up the new agency and launching it with a minimum of confusion and delay.

STAFFING THE NEW AGENCY

In selecting his staff, General Quesada made one gesture which pleased industry. He had job descriptions of his proposed top staff mimeographed and circulated widely among the airlines and the aircraft manufacturing companies. A covering letter emphasized that the new agency would need the very best people that could be found and all recruiting assistance would be appreciated. It was his desire to tap all promising sources of recruitment, both in and out of the government, so that the best man might be found for each position from among an outstanding list of candidates.

In the end, very few, if any, top jobs were filled as a result of this unusual recruiting effort, but General Quesada's letter did help dispel fears that he would take the easiest way out of his staffing problems by recruiting former military comrades. Most of the men needed came from within the ranks of the CAA, or from other government agencies.

For general counsel, Administrator Quesada recruited Daggett H. Howard from the Air Force, where he had been deputy general counsel. A graduate of Yale Law School, Mr. Howard was skilled in aviation law and had formerly served as general counsel to the Civil Aeronautics Board. For the critical job of director of the Bureau of Flight Standards, Quesada picked William B. Davis, a veteran of twenty years with the Civil Aeronautics Administration. Mr. Davis had studied at both the Harvard Graduate School of Business Administration and the Massachusetts Institute of Technology after his graduation from Tufts College and had served as a naval aviator until 1938. For the equally important job of director of the Bureau of Air Traffic Management, Quesada selected David D. Thomas, another twenty-year veteran of the CAA. Mr. Thomas began his aviation work in 1938 as an assistant controller in the Pittsburgh air route traffic control center, and at the time of his appointment was director of the Office of Air Traffic Control. He had been educated at the University of Tennessee and George Washington University School of Business Administration.

To help with the administrative problems of his agency, General Quesada drafted Alan L. Dean from the Bureau of the Budget, where Dean had been responsible for overseeing the establishment of the National Aeronautics and Space Administration. Mr. Dean had served as Bureau of the Budget adviser to the Aviation Facilities Study Group, headed by William Barclay Harding, and also as an aide to Edward P. Curtis, Presidential assistant for Aviation Facilities Planning. Mr. Dean, who held degrees from Reed University and American University, had actively participated in the legislative planning which led first to the establishment of the Airways Modernization Board and then the Federal Aviation Agency.

In only one, less important, area did Quesada fail to find an outstandingly qualified person. His recruiting brochure listed a $14,000–$16,000 job, bearing the title "Chief, Office of Public Affairs." CAA's Office of Public Affairs had over the years been the subject of turbulent resignations and transfers to Alaskan posts. At the time FAA took over, the CAA Office of Public Affairs was again rent by dissension. Quesada wisely decided not to build his new public information organization on the dubious foundations of this strife-torn office. His search for a public relations man from outside the government finally culminated in the appointment of a television writer recommended by the White House, who proved less than satisfactory as a public affairs administrator. This unfortunate choice caused many problems for the administrator, the FAA staff, and the press, but it did no permanent harm, because Administrator Quesada turned out to be as good a public affairs officer as anyone he could have hired. Despite private and public criticism from such responsible members of the Washington press corps as Bob Serling, aviation editor for United Press International, novelist, and author of several books on air safety, Quesada on the whole enjoyed good relations with most of the working aviation newsmen in Washington.

FUNCTIONS OF THE FAA

General Quesada drew almost no press criticism for his decision, while still a special assistant to President Eisenhower, to work for abolishment of the Air Coordinating Committee, which he chaired. In his 1960 report to the President, Administrator Quesada summed up his feeling about the Air Coordinating Committee, which he had long believed to be a bottleneck rather than an instrument for getting things done: "The ungainly Air Coordinating Committee which had attempted with but meager success to provide a substitute for a comprehensive aviation agency has been abolished by executive order and has disappeared from the scene. In its place FAA has taken the initiative to establish workable procedures and liaison arrangements to facilitate cooperation in aviation matters in which other agencies have significant interest."

In addition to formally abolishing the Civil Aeronautics Administration and the Airways Modernization Board, the Federal Aviation Act took away several functions from the Civil Aeronautics Board and gave them to the new Federal Aviation Agency. The basic change caused by the adoption of the Act was the transfer of safety regulatory powers, which the CAB had exercised under Title 6 of the Civil Aeronautics Act, to the administrator of the Federal Aviation Agency. In this transfer, the CAB gave up such powers as the prescribing of standards for airworthiness of civil aircraft and for the competency of airmen. CAB also gave up its authority to prescribe operating practices of air carriers and the authority to issue air traffic rules. The basic concern of the CAB in safety rule making was protected in a provision of the Federal Aviation Act which recognized the board's standing as an interested party in safety rule making and other proceedings in these fields conducted by the FAA administrator. The board also continued to be responsible for considering air safety factors in its economic rule making under Section 102 (b) and (e) of the Federal Aviation Act.

Upon accepting appointment as FAA administrator on November 1, 1958, General Quesada issued a conciliatory statement intended to quiet fears that an interregnum might occur in the change-over of aviation safety activities and responsibilities from the CAA to the new agency. "The earlier we proceed with the organization of this vital agency, the sooner the nation will benefit," Administrator Quesada said in what amounted to an order of the day. He emphasized that the operation of air traffic control towers, the certification of aircraft and airmen, and the modernization and installation of new aviation safety facilities must continue without disruption. In his order of the day, he announced that the CAA organization, including CAA Administrator James Pyle, would continue to operate undisturbed until December 31, 1958, and the same would be true of the Airways Modernization Board.

Thus no time was lost in getting the Federal Aviation Agency off to a fast start. In terms of achievement, the agency's first year of existence was in fact an outstanding one. FAA succeeded in putting together an effective organization out of the various elements that were brought together under the new Federal Aviation Act. At the same time, under the mandate from Congress to improve the federal government's management of airspace, particularly in regard to air safety, the FAA promptly launched a whole series of new programs and policies.

Such a coordinated attack on the growing number of air safety problems was long overdue. Prior to the establishment of FAA, the nation's air traffic control capability had progressively suffered from a lack of coordinated and intensive research as well as a lack of top-level executive attention, which had resulted from the fact that the CAA was a sub-agency of the Department of Commerce. Before the establishment of FAA, federal responsibility for the writing of safety rules and regulations, for allocating and regulating airspace, for managing air traffic, and for research and development were divided up among the CAA, the CAB, and the Airways Modernization Board. As early as 1948, the Air Coordinating Committee had warned that the techniques and tools available for control of the growing volume of civil air traffic were marginal at best, even by pre–World War II standards. This problem became more acute during the early and middle 1950's, when federal airways became more and more congested, as larger and faster aircraft were introduced in commercial service.

Growing concern over safety in the air had prompted Congress to pass the act setting up the FAA; the same concern led President Eisenhower to appoint General Elwood Quesada as head of the new agency. Before we consider in detail the main functions of the FAA, let us for a moment examine the personalities as well as the roles played by General Quesada and the two administrators who succeeded him.

III

FAA's Three Administrators

Elwood R. "Pete" Quesada is a native of Washington, D.C. During World War II, General Quesada's jobs ranged from commanding general of the Ninth Fighter Command in England to assistant chief of the Air Staff in charge of intelligence. His decorations included the Purple Heart and the Air Medal with two silver clusters. After retiring as an Air Force lieutenant general in 1951, General Quesada was for a time vice-president and general manager of the Missile Systems Division of the Lockheed Aircraft Corporation.

THE FAA UNDER QUESADA

With his military training and experience as a command pilot and aviation officer, it was inevitable that General Quesada would bring with him to the job of FAA administrator some of the habits of a lifetime. Not only did he bring a command approach to administration, but he refused to treat airline pilots—traditionally considered the monarchs of the airways—with the deference that some previous CAA administrators had led them to expect was their due.

In his book *The Probable Cause*, United Press International aviation editor Bob Serling sums up some of the differences of opinion that existed between General Quesada and the airline pilots:

Personalities were involved as well as politics, unfortunately. Pete Quesada was a devoted, efficient public servant who also happened to be short-tempered, undiplomatic and, on occasions, admittedly arbitrary. Pilots are devoted, professionally efficient, and also happen to be immensely proud to the point of occasional shortsightedness. Neither Quesada nor the average airline captain was the type to admit wholeheartedly and without reservation that the other guy may be right at least some of the time. The tragedy of the feud was that, actually, both sides were simultaneously right and wrong in certain respects. No one quarreled with Quesada's determination to protect the public, and no one denies that, under its rock-hard chief, FAA made definite strides toward air safety. But there is something to be said for the airline pilots too. Many of the rules and regulations on the books today were put there at pilot insistence; many of aviation's needed reforms stemmed from pilot experience and pressure.

Shortly after he took over as administrator of FAA, Administrator Quesada tightened up the rules on cockpit discipline. The new rules ran into immediate opposition from the Air Line Pilots Association. The association's president, Clancy Sayen—who was to die in a tragic air crash only a few years later—accused the FAA not only of tightening up the rules stating how long a captain could properly be absent from his flight deck duties, but also of filing violation reports against airline captains who were absent from their post for as little as seven minutes. Despite such complaints, FAA did not back down. Administrator Quesada told Captain Sayen, "The FAA will not be threatened into retreat." He pointed out two specific instances, in which captains had been fined for being absent from their duties in the cockpit and endangering the lives of 154 people aboard their planes. One case involved an autopilot that went haywire over the North Atlantic and pushed the plane into a near-fatal dive. The other case involved a near-collision between a DC-7 and an Air Force tanker aircraft.

Quesada encountered some mild criticism of his new rule

from the Flight Safety Foundation. The foundation recommended that pilots, particularly on long flights, be allowed to get up out of their seats at least once an hour to restore circulation and maintain alertness. The FAA, however, maintained that a pilot must never leave the cockpit except to use the toilet.

In his book *The Probable Cause,* Serling reports the case of an airline captain who was asked by the stewardess to help open the door to the liquor cabinet, which had become jammed. The captain looked at the stewardess for a moment, then picked up the public address microphone and said, "Ladies and gentlemen, this is the captain speaking. I am informed that the stewardess cannot open the liquor cabinet which is stuck. Inasmuch as Mr. Quesada has decreed that pilots cannot leave the flight deck except in cases of emergency, we will be unable to serve drinks before dinner. Thank you."

Before Administrator Quesada had finished his fight with the pilots over cabin discipline, he plunged into a second heated controversy when he approved a new rule that prohibited airline pilots sixty years old or over from commanding transport aircraft (the age limit was fifty-five for jets). FAA's reason for this rule was that medical evidence had showed a greater likelihood of heart attacks after age sixty, and that pilots fifty-five years of age were having too much difficulty transitioning to jet aircraft after a lifetime of flying the slower piston-engine planes.

The airline pilots also attacked this rule, even to the extent of challenging it in the federal courts on the grounds that it was arbitrary and capricious, and that the FAA had no evidence to prove that the age of a captain bore any relationship to airline accidents. If anything, said the Air Line Pilots Association, older pilots had better safety records than the younger ones. Furthermore, every known case of an accident caused by a pilot having a heart attack involved pilots who were *under* fifty-five years of age. The association suggested that the way to solve the problem of possible incapacitation of a pilot was to require that a third pilot be carried aboard all large transport planes.

Despite the airline pilots' efforts, legal and otherwise, to block the new age rule, the FAA put its ban on sixty-year-old command pilots into effect on March 15, 1960, emphasizing that the purpose of the rule was not to correct past problems but to anticipate future ones and to take corrective measures before air tragedies occurred. The court sustained the FAA and the Air Line Pilots Association retreated, but not without a certain bitterness, which lingers even to this day.

When General Quesada announced his resignation as FAA administrator, he was ushered out of office with a bitter blast from one of the most powerful pressure groups in aviation—the Aircraft Owners and Pilots Association (AOPA). With a membership of more than 130,000 pilots and plane owners, the association was, and continues to be, a force to be reckoned with by any FAA administrator. An editorial in the December, 1960, issue of *The AOPA Pilot* summed up that organization's opinion of General Quesada as FAA administrator:

> The Quesada type of operation has left deep marks that will take a long time removing. Much must be done to correct the FAA. First and foremost, of course, are the new administrator and deputy administrator. Both must be dedicated public servants and true civilians, not professional military men in civilian clothes. Then the most searching, hardheaded examination of the entire colossal agency must be put into operation immediately, with the primary view of protecting the public. Under the guise of safety, deliberately fanned by the FAA itself with a variety of scare techniques designed to keep an uninformed Congress and public on edge, the FAA has spread itself to the point that it is costing the public $9,519.75 per active civil airplane per year. And it's no wonder, what with gigantic research and development funds, a five-million-dollar medical

boondoggle in Oklahoma, more than 40,000 employees, and enormous other extravagances so often hidden in complex appropriation bills.

The Aircraft Owners and Pilots Association advised General Quesada's successor to end what it called the Napoleonic code (you are guilty until you prove yourself innocent), and recommended that the new administrator take whatever steps were necessary to assure all American citizens who fly a fair and impartial hearing in any matters involving the FAA. The association urged the new administrator to change the rules for medical examinations so that third-class medical certificates (necessary for private and student licenses) could be issued on the endorsement of any properly licensed doctor of medicine, and not just doctors who held FAA appointment. It also recommended elimination of all military personnel in key administrative positions, except those needed to look out for the immediate interests of the military in FAA functions that bear directly on military operations.

In only one respect did President John F. Kennedy follow the advice of the Aircraft Owners and Pilots Association: he did appoint a civilian to replace General Quesada. The new FAA administrator did make some reduction in the FAA budget, but the FAA-designated medical examiner requirement continues to this day. And many of the new administrator's safety activities, such as the dramatic crash tests of obsolete transport aircraft, were more frightening, from the industry's viewpoint, than anything Administrator Quesada's staff had ever thought up.

General Quesada was an articulate defender of his policies and actions. In his transmittal letter to the President, which accompanied the second annual report of the FAA, he answered some of the criticisms made of the FAA during its first two years. As a preface to his remarks, he described briefly the legislative history of the Federal Aviation Act "to help put in unmistakable context the regulatory activities of the FAA over the past two years." He reminded the President that the House Committee on Interstate and Foreign Commerce had released a report in August, 1957, *Air Transportation and Air Space Use,* containing the statement:

> Testimony taken by your Committee this Session, and during the 84th Congress, points clearly to the need for greater attention to safety measures, both on the part of government agencies and industry. Any tendency by agencies to proceed with caution in promulgating or enforcing regulations to promote safety must be avoided at all cost, even at the risk of being charged with undue harshness.

Administrator Quesada noted that less than a year later the Aviation Subcommittee of the Senate Interstate and Foreign Commerce Committee, in favorably reporting the bill which would later become the Federal Aviation Act, took a similar position, characterizing "the ever-greater exploitation of this buoyant resource aloft" as an enduring aspect of the American frontier. "And, unfortunately," the subcommittee added, "the frontier still appears to be as much in need of law and order as ever."

These and other documents bearing on the legislative history of the Federal Aviation Act made it clear that Congress would stand for "no half-hearted administration of the law." Accordingly, on the very first day of FAA's existence, the rule-making procedures that had existed in the predecessor agencies were revised. The new procedures, said the FAA administrator, guarantee the opportunity for all interested persons, as well as the public at large, to present their views on proposed rules before they are adopted. They ensure that the agency's regulatory actions will be fair and in the best interest of the aviation industry as well as the public. They "also protect the rule-making process from *ex parte* influence and expressly recognize that public interest in air safety requires an open record, free of such influence."

Quesada did not identify any particular special interest

group, but he told the President that "despite calculated efforts on the part of certain special interests to misrepresent the procedural safeguards contained in the basic Act, it is a fact that the laws of all safety regulatory agencies in the transportation field provide less opportunity for legal review of their action than that provided for in the Federal Aviation Act." In his two years as administrator, the agency had adopted many new and important measures to bring the safety regulations into step with the requirements of present-day aviation. This new safety program of the agency involved scores of rule-making actions, "yet to date, although several legal challenges of our rule-making actions have been attempted, none has been successful in attacking either their reasonableness or their compliance with procedural due process."

General Quesada, in his report, called attention to the fact that the first appraisal made by the new FAA staff revealed that no comprehensive revision of medical standards for airmen had been undertaken for thirty-four years.

In that span of time revolutionary changes have taken place in the art of aerodynamics, while medical science in its wonderful march forward has brought into being an entirely new field of application—aviation medicine. We felt that an aggressive medical program offered a most promising approach to positive achievements in safety. Accordingly, we set on foot a vigorous aeromedical research and medical standards program and improved procedures for the administration of medical examination of airmen.

In 1960, FAA established a Bureau of Aviation Medicine to replace the former Office of the Air Surgeon. In addition, Quesada appointed a number of leading forensic pathologists as consultants to FAA to determine to what extent human factors were related to aircraft accidents.

The agency had also discovered that certain proficiency standards for airmen needed extensive revision to bring them into step with the increasing complexity of modern air-craft and current flying environments. Turbojet passenger service was inaugurated by U.S. carriers in October, 1958, only three months before the FAA began its review of safety regulations. By the end of 1959, the airlines had a fleet of 84 pure jets, and during 1960 they began operating 120 additional pure jet aircraft. By the summer of 1960, more than half of all scheduled airline passenger miles in the United States were being flown by turbine-powered aircraft. According to General Quesada, FAA's initial review of aviation safety indicated that "ultimately the entire regulatory structure must be recodified, simplified, and made more compatible with the present responsibility of the agency and more useful for the aviation industry." Such a sweeping review would require several years to complete.

In the meantime, the FAA was directing its attention to priority safety needs. Among early actions taken were the rewriting of rules to require some instrument flight instruction for private pilots, a flight test demonstration of ability to control aircraft, demonstration of a planned cross-country flight for all pilots, and familiarity with the use of radio for communications and navigation by both private and commercial pilots. New rules also required that the FAA give its approval to air carrier flight crew training programs; another early rule raised the qualification level for copilots serving as second in command on air carrier aircraft.

From an equipment standpoint, a first priority safety item had been the installation of airborne weather radar in transport category aircraft. Another early priority requirement called for all large turbine-powered aircraft to carry flight recorders which could be used, in the event of an accident, to reconstruct the final minutes of the aircraft's pattern of flight.

"Regulations once adopted must be enforced," Quesada told the President.

If those to whom Congress has entrusted the task fail to uphold with impartiality the supremacy of law and order, effective government breaks down. It has never been our practice to allow anarchy to flourish in the nation's navigable airspace. During the early months following the FAA's establishment we became increasingly concerned over complacency or laxness in two vital areas of safety: crew and cockpit discipline and aircraft maintenance. The emphasis of our enforcement, surveillance and inspection efforts has accordingly been toward bringing to light and correcting as rapidly as possible deficiencies in these areas.

This increased emphasis on compliance resulted in the filing of 3,822 violations during calendar year 1959; an estimated 5,000 violation notices were filed in calendar year 1960. Before the establishment of the FAA, the yearly average of violation notices issued by CAA was about 2,000.

HALABY AND THE "FRIENDLY AVIATION AGENCY"

With the change from President Eisenhower's Administration to that of President Kennedy came a corresponding shift in administrators of FAA. To replace General Quesada, the President-elect chose a California lawyer, businessman, and former test pilot, Najeeb E. Halaby. In his own way, "Jeeb" Halaby turned out to be as colorful a personality as was Pete Quesada. But while Quesada usually tried to stay above and a little ahead of the strife and turmoil that marked many of FAA's key decisions, Administrator Halaby could almost always be found in the thick of the battle.

In an announcement of a speech by Administrator Halaby given on May 23, 1961, the Aero Club of Washington told its members: "In scanning his biography one gets the impression he is a half dozen people at least. It shows him as a pilot, businessman, financier, government official, industrial corporation executive, hunter, tennis player, golfer, father of three, and even a Texan."

Born in Texas on November 19, 1915, Mr. Halaby was a graduate of Stanford University and the Yale Law School. He got his pilot's license at seventeen, bought a plane, and liked flying so much he became a commercial pilot. During World War II, he was a civilian instructor for the Army Air Corps, a Lockheed test pilot, and a naval aviator. He flight-tested the first U.S. jet, the Bell P-59, and made the first continuous transcontinental jet-powered flight. In 1948 and 1949 he served as an assistant to Secretary of Defense James Forrestal. In 1953, he was selected by the U.S. Junior Chamber of Commerce for the Arthur Flemming award as "outstanding young man in federal service." In 1954, he left the government, resigning from his position as Deputy Assistant of Defense for International Security Affairs. Just before being picked by President Kennedy to run the FAA, he was secretary-treasurer of Aerospace Corporation, El Segundo, California.

Being a civilian, and a particularly well qualified one, Halaby had no difficulty gaining Senate confirmation for the job of FAA administrator. As one of President Kennedy's New Frontiersmen, Administrator Halaby took over his new job with enthusiasm. During his first year, major policy studies were completed, and the agency was reorganized. Halaby's concern with the agency's poor relationship with pilots in general and private and business pilots in particular resulted in a major effort to improve communications and earn the good will of the aviation community.

As the FAA began its third year of operation, Administrator Halaby reported that, despite many significant achievements, a gap still existed between aviation's mounting need for services and the government's capacity to serve. At Halaby's prompting, President Kennedy ordered the establishment of two task forces—Projects Horizon and Beacon. The Project Horizon group reported in September, 1961, on a broad range of national aviation goals through the year

1967. Two months later, the Beacon group submitted recommendations for an orderly and economic evaluation of the existing system of air traffic control. The system was being expertly operated, but it was outmoded and in need of improvement. To cope with the increasingly complex patterns of civil and military traffic, the future air traffic control system, including weather, communications, airspace utilization, and airport subsystems, should be developed as a single system concept. To implement this recommendation with specific proposals, FAA organized a systems design team consisting of thirteen FAA experts and one representative from the Department of Defense.

Administrator Halaby focused his attention, not only on internal FAA administrative problems and long-range planning, but also on the friction areas where FAA touched the private flying community, commercial aviation, and military aviation. In an effort to develop the image of a "Friendly Aviation Agency," Halaby made frequent swings around the country, meeting with airmen in what he called "hangar flying" sessions. These were free-swinging question-and-answer periods, open to any pilot or other person interested in aviation. Anybody could ask any question and be assured of a straight-from-the-shoulder answer from the Big Boss himself.

This highly democratic approach won Jeeb Halaby many friends among pilots and others in the general aviation community. It did not, however, win him many friends on Capitol Hill, for congressmen are notoriously suspicious of appointed federal officials who invade their districts for any reason, particularly for the purpose of making friends and possibly influencing voters. It was on one of his good-will trips to southern Texas—the state, ironically, where Halaby was born—that the friendly aviation administrator inadvertently made an enemy more powerful than any of the friends he made through his barnstorming efforts. In a casual and private discussion with a San Antonio city official, Halaby criticized the district's first-term congressman, Henry Gonzalez, who had been trying to make a public issue out of his attempts to keep FAA from closing an air traffic control center in his district. Halaby's remark—something to the effect that Representative Gonzalez was acting like a typical freshman congressman in his effort to attract votes by attacking the big, bad Federal Aviation Agency—was repeated by the city official at a press conference. Being too honest to deny that he had said what in fact he had said, Halaby could only explain, rather inadequately, that he had said it in confidence.* This public admission served to make Representative Gonzalez even more angry at Administrator Halaby. The enemy thus made was a formidable one. Representative Gonzalez was one of the first congressmen of Mexican descent and thus commanded strong emotional loyalties among his South Texas constituents. He also had a powerful friend in the then Vice-President of the United States, Lyndon B. Johnson. When Johnson was a senator from Texas, he had given active assistance to the young congressman. Despite repeated and sincere efforts to patch up his differences with Congressman Gonzalez, Najeeb Halaby was never able to recover from this political fumble.

As recently as February, 1965, for example, Representative Gonzalez introduced a bill to prohibit the closing of any federal installation by any federal agency without prior public hearing. "Recent events," Gonzalez said, "have shown the need for the people to have a right to a public hearing on a contemplated shutdown of an installation in their commu-

---

* In a letter to the author, received as this volume was going to press, Representative Gonzalez, who was asked to comment on the foregoing account of his disagreement with Halaby, wrote: "I would not call his criticism of me as being 'in confidence.' There are radio and TV tapes at the stations in San Antonio which reveal exactly how he conducted himself during his short visit to San Antonio. He was rude and arrogant and topped it all off by saying that he didn't have time to get involved in a dispute between 'two cow towns' (San Antonio and Houston)."

nity." So long as they do not have this right, entire communities "will remain exposed to the whims and designs of appointed administrators, some of whom may be petty tyrants, more interested in the advancement of their own careers than the advancement of public welfare."

Najeeb Halaby's test pilot days were far behind him when he took over as FAA administrator, but flying was still in his blood and whenever possible he took the controls. He found using one of his fleet of FAA planes to be the most interesting and pleasant way to travel. This lead to a humorous and typical Halaby incident. On a pleasant fall day, while taxiing the FAA's "Nan One"—at that time a Grumman Gulfstream executive turboprop—Halaby, who was carrying with him the CAB chairman and a staff of accident investigators on their way to a crash, brushed wing tips with a United Air Lines Viscount that was standing in the run-up area. The Viscount was awaiting take-off clearance, when Halaby's attention was diverted, and the left wing tip of "Nan One" briefly brushed the right wing tip of the Viscount. Damage to both wing tips was minor, but a violation report was filed against Mr. N. E. Halaby, 1711 New York Avenue, Washington 25, D.C. In due course, on December 18, 1962, the aforementioned airman received a violation notice from the regional counsel of the Federal Aviation Agency in New York, recounting the sequence of events which led to the accident (see Appendix D). The violation notice continued: "The foregoing indicates that you failed to exercise the care and caution required of the holder of a pilot certificate and consequently, that your operation was contrary to Section 60.12 of the Civil Air Regulations and Section 610(a) of the Federal Aviation Act of 1958 (number 72 Stat. 780)."

For failing to exercise the necessary care and caution, a pilot may be fined up to $1,000 in the form of a civil penalty. The FAA is also authorized under its regulations to accept a lesser sum in compromise of the penalty. As a consequence of this proviso, Mr. Halaby was advised that if he were prepared to offer $50 in full settlement of the civil penalty, this would be acceptable. The small sum—the same as for any ordinary pilot—was based on the fact, as noted in a regional counsel's letter, that Halaby had "acknowledged full responsibility; that safety of flight operations was not compromised and that in your previous twenty-eight years of flying, you have not been involved in any accident or cited for violation of safety regulations."

Even though President Johnson and Najeeb Halaby are native sons of Texas, there have long been differences of opinion between the two men, which run deeper than Halaby's clash with Johnson's friend, Representative Gonzalez. While still Vice-President, Johnson had been named by President Kennedy to head the White House Supersonic Transport Advisory Group. In general, both Administrator Halaby and Vice-President Johnson—Johnson more than Halaby—favored going ahead with a government-financed program to build a 2,000-mile-an-hour commercial air transport. But both men are stubborn and not easily swayed by argument—rather, they both pride themselves on their ability to sway others through the force of their personalities.

Halaby's impatience with many basic political facts of life did not sit well with the then Vice-President, who was, and is, highly politically oriented. Nor did President Johnson take kindly to Halaby's decision to leave government service as soon as the President could find a suitable replacement. The President decided to take his time; he wanted a particular man for the FAA job and was in no hurry to accept the resignation tendered by Mr. Halaby. Instead, he ordered the FAA administrator to undertake a special mission to Russia.

President Johnson, like President Kennedy, was hopeful that the U.S. might establish better trade relations with Russia as a further step toward peace. The Russians, for their part, had been seeking for several years to obtain commercial air traffic rights between Moscow and New York. A number of technical problems existed in connection with this route, revolving in part around the differences in Russian and U.S. navigation aids, as well as air traffic control procedures. President Johnson ordered Mr. Halaby to go to Moscow and confer with the Russians about these technical difficulties, which had to be cleared up before a route agreement could take effect, and also to sound out the Russians in both the political and economic areas.

Administrator Halaby elected to fly to Moscow in the FAA's four-engine executive plane, a Lockheed Jet Star. Mr. Halaby took with him a small technical staff and a State Department representative. At the suggestion of the State Department, he also took along Mrs. Halaby, which occasioned some criticism on Capitol Hill, particularly among those who thought that the very limited number of seats in the plane should have been filled with a few more Soviet experts.

But in the end it did not matter who filled the seats, for the trip accomplished little more than to provide U.S. intelligence evaluators with a professional test pilot's opinion of a number of Soviet commercial aircraft. While en route to Moscow, Halaby tested the Russian acceptance of small aircraft in the Berlin Corridor. Halaby's report to President Johnson on his return from Moscow was never made public.

He did, however, discuss his trip privately with a small group of newsmen after his return. He had found the Russians very anxious to open a commercial air route to the United States. He had flown the TU-114 from the copilot's seat and reported that it had a 350,000-pound maximum take-off weight (compared to 314,000 pounds for the Boeing 707) and carried 224 passengers (compared to about 210 passengers for the largest U.S. jets). The navigation aid system used by the Russians was somewhat out of date by present world standards, but before the United States began flying to Moscow, they intended to install the latest equipment. Mr. Halaby had discussed the supersonic transport with several Soviet designers and had got the clear impression that they did not intend merely to dress up a bomber and call it a supersonic transport in order to score another "first." In fact, the Russian approach was very similar to that of the United States. They expected to have their prototype aircraft flying in the 1970's.

Halaby marked time after his return from Moscow, but one clear indication of his growing lack of rapport with the new Administration—arising out of his insistence on leaving the FAA—was the mauling that his spending estimates took during preliminary discussions with the Bureau of the Budget. Halaby had to appeal personally to the President before some of the more crippling cuts could be restored and a minimal "bare bones" budget could be sent to Congress.

It was about this time that rumors began circulating that he had been offered a top executive position with Pan American World Airways, but Halaby denied this, declaring that so long as he was FAA administrator, he was definitely not job-hunting. All during the early months of 1965, Halaby continued to deny rumors of his impending departure. Then on April 27, a White House press announcement brought the uncertainty to an end; the President had decided to replace Mr. Halaby with a retired Air Force general.

WILLIAM McKEE—THIRD ADMINISTRATOR

At 11:27 A.M. eastern daylight time, on July 1, 1965, President Lyndon Johnson formally swore in FAA Administrator William F. McKee. The President was in particularly good humor on this occasion and had some kind words to say about the departing administrator:

Jeeb Halaby gave up the quiet, everyday pleasures of being a test pilot to face the perils and the dangers of bureaucratic life in Washington. But every passenger who flies across the country in a plane owes him a deep debt of personal gratitude. In four years of dedicated, tireless service he has done much to assure public confidence in the safety of air travel. By the inspiration of his vigorous leadership he has greatly advanced the performance of the fine agency that he has headed.

The reason for General McKee's appointment was made clear in a private memorandum that John W. Macy, Sr., Civil Service Commission Chairman and chief executive recruiter for the President, prepared for President Johnson on April 27, 1965:

As in the case of your selection of Admiral Raborn to head CIA, I believe you would be well advised to turn to a distinguished military officer to succeed Najeeb Halaby as Administrator of the Federal Aviation Agency. I recommend General William F. McKee, who retired last year with four-star rank as Vice-Chief of Staff of the Air Force. For more than nine years General McKee has served as Vice-Commander and Commander of the total Air Force materiel operation, administering the expenditure of a significant portion of the Defense budget for the procurement of essential aircraft and supporting services. His record of service clearly demonstrates his leadership ability, his managerial skills and his knowledge of aviation. Secretary McNamara advised, "In my 22 years of general association with General McKee, in a variety of roles, I have considered him to be one of the strongest managers in the service of his country." Since his military retirement, General McKee has been assisting the NASA leadership in important phases of the space program.

General McKee, a West Point graduate, was commissioned in the Coast Artillery Corps in 1929. After a series of overseas and domestic assignments, he joined Army Air Force Headquarters in 1942, and afterwards served both in the states and overseas in Air Force logistic and transport operations. His service record is unique in that he is the only Air Force general to achieve four-star rank without ever having been a pilot. Commenting on his appointment, *Aviation Daily* said on April 29, 1965, "Although little known in civil aviation, General William F. McKee will move into his new post of FAA administrator with a reputation as a management specialist and a reasonable man. In personality, the successor to Najeeb Halaby is undramatic and gives the impression of being less forceful than he actually is. He is a good public speaker. One NASA associate characterized McKee as 'not a wave-maker; he works quietly and efficiently.' "

In an interview given the author shortly before the Senate confirmed McKee in his new post, the general said that he thought not being a pilot might have its advantages, since he would not automatically presume that he knew all about aviation matters and would be willing to listen to pilots as well as anyone else that might have sound views and the required information. General McKee always tried to surround himself with good advisers, and to listen to them. He told a story about his late father, a doctor who spent his lifetime in general practice at Saltsville, Virginia. During the war, his father would occasionally come to Washington. One evening when the general returned home tired and dispirited, his father wanted to know why he was feeling so low. General McKee said he had spent the entire day in meetings in which everybody talked and talked and not too much was accomplished, whereon his father quoted an old jingle:

> A wise old owl lived in an oak;
> The more he saw the less he spoke;
> The less he spoke, the more he heard.
> Why can't we all be like that wise old bird?

This bit of old-fashioned doggerel made a deep impression on the general. He promptly committed it to memory and has used it as a guide ever since. The Library of Congress has been unable to identify the author of these four lines; however, it claims that the quotation was often used by John D. Rockefeller, Sr., and that President Calvin Coolidge was reported to have had it cut into the stone mantle of his fireplace in his Northampton, Massachusetts, home.

Following his father's advice and listening while others talked has earned McKee at least one award: Air Force General Hap Arnold presented him with a set of "honorary" observer's wings while he was serving as assistant chief of the Air Staff.

General McKee was well known and well liked on Capitol Hill, so his appointment encountered a minimum of opposition. When President Johnson announced that he wanted General McKee to be able to draw his full retirement pay while also drawing the pay of FAA administrator, the response on the Hill was one of muted protest only, rather than outright opposition to the President's highly unusual request. The job of FAA administrator is classified at Level I in the executive establishment, which means a salary of $30,-000 a year, $5,000 more than the members of Congress are paid, but $5,000 less than the Chief Justice of the United States. By comparison, the Vice-President of the United States and the Speaker of the House each earn $43,000 a year; President Johnson is paid $100,000. Since no one else in government is permitted to draw two salary checks, General McKee is, as can be seen, one of the highest paid officials on the federal payroll.

Administrator McKee is hard-working, energetic, and even-tempered. He has long since mastered the art of government administration. His assistants have learned that he is a very quick decision-maker, and it is not necessary to use the FAA morning staff meeting to take up matters awaiting decision from the administrator. They have learned, too, to deal with their boss on the basis of a memo of one or two pages, which contains the arguments both for and against a course of action, and a final recommendation as to what should be done. For the most part, his aides say, Administrator McKee goes along with the staff recommendations.

When Administrator McKee is asked to define the goals of his agency, he is fond of quoting the introduction of the Federal Aviation Act. He often says that he feels that the agency's primary responsibility is air safety. Its secondary responsibility is public service. He limits his travels, whenever possible, to a jet flight out in the morning and another back in the evening. Using this quick hop technique, by the end of his first year on the job, he had visited all of his regional offices and a good number of his traffic control centers.

One of his major responsibilities as FAA administrator is the supersonic transport (SST) program. It is a rare day in the life of the FAA administrator when he does not deal with some SST matter. He has visited the principal contractors involved in the design program, and regional directors keep in touch with headquarters by means of a Monday 1:30 P.M. conference telephone call. This call uses circuits that the agency leases for emergency stand-by use. It is both a communication check and a general conference of administrators not only in the continental United States but also in Alaska and Hawaii and the chief European FAA offices. The heads of the Atlantic City research center and the FAA installations in Oklahoma City are also on the line during these weekly calls. General McKee does not monitor the calls except under unusual circumstances; the one-hour conferences are almost always presided over by the deputy administrator. General McKee's communication system includes a daily "alert bulletin," covering all aviation accidents, incidents, near-misses, and other bits of intelligence that flow in through the twenty-four-hour-a-day communication center, which keeps in touch with every control tower operated by the FAA in the United States.

McKee's sense of humor has endeared him to the aviation industry. On October 26, 1965, he began a speech to the Aero

Club of Washington by saying: "I want to begin today with an announcement. I won't be talking as a student. I was somewhat astonished by your announcement that I was taking flying lessons. The only time I could learn to fly, even if it were a good thing, which I doubt, would be between midnight and reveille. So I am not learning to fly. And that may be good news for the aviation industry."

Further along in the same speech, Administrator McKee said:

We in the FAA shall adhere to one simple dictum: if it is compatible with our mission of promoting safety and the public interest we shall do it. If it is not, we shall not do it. . . . Probably the best asset we have, in addition to our people, is the fine organization developed by General Quesada and Jeeb Halaby. After these three months as FAA administrator, I have some understanding of the problems Pete Quesada faced in forming the agency. I also have some understanding of the problems Jeeb Halaby faced in succeeding Quesada. I should like here to pay tribute to both of these dedicated men for their contributions and good work.

It is this strong feeling for the diplomatic phrase that has made Géneral McKee the least controversial of the three FAA administrators. And it is his sense of duty to his superiors—the President in particular—that made it easy for Administrator McKee to support the establishment of the Department of Transportation in 1966, even though this meant the end of an independent FAA, and the downgrading, by one notch, of the job of FAA administrator.

IV

Organization and Functions Today

The administrator and the deputy administrator of the Federal Aviation Administration are appointed by the President, with the advice and consent of the Senate. Associate administrators, whose administrative responsibilities are depicted in the accompanying chart, are appointed by the administrator, as are regional directors, directors of services, and other major officials of the agency.

The FAA operates in the field through eight regional directors. Each is responsible for FAA activities within the geographic boundary of the region. Headquarters for the eastern region is New York's Kennedy International Airport, Jamaica, Long Island; the southern region has its headquarters in Atlanta, Georgia; the southwest region in Fort Worth, Texas; the central region, Kansas City, Missouri; and the Western region in Los Angeles, California. The Alaska region, which includes the Aleutian Islands, has its headquarters at Anchorage, Alaska. The Pacific region, which covers Hawaii, Wake Island, Canton Island, and Guam, is headquartered in Honolulu.

The FAA also maintains a regional headquarters in Brussels, Belgium. This office supervises the flight-checking of overseas navigational aids and maintains liaison with the aviation authorities of foreign governments, international organizations, and foreign manufacturers. The region's responsibility includes Europe, Africa, and the Middle East.

Exclusive of the supersonic transport program, the FAA budget averages just under $750 million annually, of which $500 million is for current agency operations and the balance divided among facilities and equipment, research and development, operation and maintenance of the two national capital airports, and the grants-in-aid of the federal airport program (see Appendix C, Summary of Budget Estimates).

Although the FAA is concerned with air safety at the source, so to speak, and tests and certificates all airmen as well as all aircraft and aircraft components, its basic air safety job is air traffic control. All aircraft that fly under instrument flight rules in the United States are subject to a single air traffic control system. This means that military and air carrier aircraft, as well as all other civil aircraft, are controlled by the same procedures, from the same facilities, and by the same agency—the Federal Aviation Administration.

To facilitate control of air traffic flying under instrument flight conditions, the FAA has established approximately 350,000 miles of federal airways and 94,000 miles of jet routes. These airways and routes are laid out as two separate systems, a lower airway system, which extends up to 18,000 feet, and a jet route system, from 18,000 to 45,000 feet. The airways are true highways of the sky, complete with their own electronic versions of marker signs, access roads, directional guides, and even parking places—areas around airports known as holding points. Flights are often instructed to hold at these parking points, flying a racetrack-shaped pattern. This enables the traffic controllers to bring waiting aircraft into airports in an orderly fashion. The air traffic control activities of FAA are described in greater detail in Chapter VI.

Airports are another key element in FAA's air safety program. For more than twenty years, under the provisions of the federal-aid-to-airports program (see Chapter IX), the

FEDERAL AV

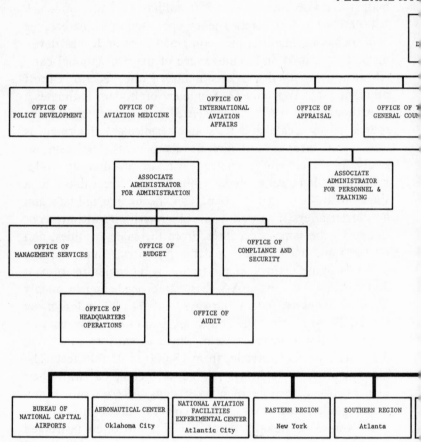

OFFICE OF POLICY DEVELOPMENT

OFFICE OF AVIATION MEDICINE

OFFICE OF INTERNATIONAL AVIATION AFFAIRS

OFFICE OF APPRAISAL

OFFICE OF GENERAL COUN

ASSOCIATE ADMINISTRATOR FOR ADMINISTRATION

ASSOCIATE ADMINISTRATOR FOR PERSONNEL & TRAINING

OFFICE OF MANAGEMENT SERVICES

OFFICE OF BUDGET

OFFICE OF COMPLIANCE AND SECURITY

OFFICE OF HEADQUARTERS OPERATIONS

OFFICE OF AUDIT

BUREAU OF NATIONAL CAPITAL AIRPORTS

AERONAUTICAL CENTER
Oklahoma City

NATIONAL AVIATION FACILITIES EXPERIMENTAL CENTER
Atlantic City

EASTERN REGION
New York

SOUTHERN REGION
Atlanta

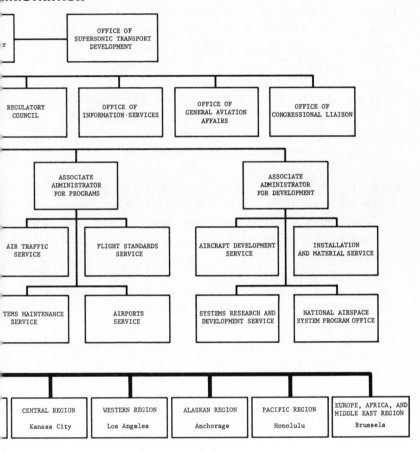

OFFICE OF
SUPERSONIC TRANSPORT
DEVELOPMENT

REGULATORY
COUNCIL

OFFICE OF
INFORMATION SERVICES

OFFICE OF
GENERAL AVIATION
AFFAIRS

OFFICE OF
CONGRESSIONAL LIAISON

ASSOCIATE
ADMINISTRATOR
FOR PROGRAMS

ASSOCIATE
ADMINISTRATOR
FOR DEVELOPMENT

AIR TRAFFIC
SERVICE

FLIGHT STANDARDS
SERVICE

AIRCRAFT DEVELOPMENT
SERVICE

INSTALLATION
AND MATERIAL SERVICE

TEMS MAINTENANCE
SERVICE

AIRPORTS
SERVICE

SYSTEMS RESEARCH AND
DEVELOPMENT SERVICE

NATIONAL AIRSPACE
SYSTEM PROGRAM OFFICE

CENTRAL REGION

Kansas City

WESTERN REGION

Los Angeles

ALASKAN REGION

Anchorage

PACIFIC REGION

Honolulu

EUROPE, AFRICA, AND
MIDDLE EAST REGION

Brussels

FAA has been providing publicly owned airports with matching funds to assist in necessary development and expansion of runways and navigational aids. In addition to its continuing efforts to expand and modernize the nation's public-use airport system, the FAA operates the two major airports serving Washington, D.C.: Washington National Airport and Dulles International Airport.

In contrast to its responsibility for the two national capital airports, which has brought a disproportionate number of headaches to the agency (as described in Chapter X), FAA's responsibility for certification of both airmen and aircraft has been discharged with an astonishingly small amount of either criticism or top management attention, probably because the procedures for certification (Chapter VII) have evolved gradually through trial and error over the years and are now so well refined that changes are infrequent and usually evolutionary.

The Federal Aviation Administration conducts an aggressive program of research and development with the primary objective of improving air safety. The portion of this effort involving tests and experimentation is conducted at the FAA National Aviation Facilities Experimental Center (NAFEC), located fifteen miles northwest of Atlantic City, New Jersey. This modern, 5,000-acre research establishment is the site of experimental work in air traffic control, weather analysis, aircraft and engine safety, airport lighting and instrumentation, communications, and navigation. The Center maintains a large simulation facility, capable of simulating a supersonic flight across the country with all the attendant air traffic problems. Thousands of hours of highly realistic air traffic simulations are performed on this facility each year. Contract work by the aviation industry, universities, foundations, and nonprofit organizations plays an essential role in the research and development program. Other aspects of the program will be discussed in Chapter VIII.

The agency also maintains the FAA Aeronautical Center at Oklahoma City, Oklahoma, which includes fifteen acres of repair shops and warehousing facilities. All FAA aircraft receive their major overhaul and modification work in the Center's service base. Approximately 5,000 FAA field offices depend on the depot at the Center for operating and maintenance supplies, which are centrally purchased and shipped in bulk to the Center for processing and distribution to facility sites.

The Aeronautical Center is also one of the largest basic training areas for aviation skills in the world. Approximately 1,500 students attend classes at the Oklahoma City FAA Academy, studying some 150 different subjects ranging from air traffic control to repair of electronic equipment. One important job of training is handled by the National Aircraft Accident Investigation School, sponsored jointly by the National Transportation Safety Board (NTSB) and the FAA. Most of the students at the school are NTSB and FAA inspectors and investigators, but men from all segments of aviation are trained in uniform accident investigation procedures. Foreign aviation accident investigators are also trained in this unique school at the Aeronautical Center.

The FAA has been active in international aviation affairs ever since it was established. It cooperates with the State Department's Agency for International Development by sending civil aviation assistance teams abroad to provide technical aid to other countries and to advise on the construction and modernization of airports and the installation of airways and aids to navigation. (See Chapter XI for a detailed description of the technical assistance program.) Under an international engineering program, FAA tests the airworthiness of foreign aircraft, using the same safety standards that apply in the United States. The agency also maintains liaison with the International Civil Aviation Organization in Montreal, through which international standards, practices, and safety procedures are multilaterally adopted so that pilots everywhere in the world may operate under the same international rules.

One of the most important functions of the FAA since 1960 has been its leadership in the development of a supersonic transport aircraft. In December of that year, the first FAA administrator, General Elwood R. Quesada, recommended "that the executive and legislative branches of our government give prompt and careful consideration to the immediate establishment of a national program for the development of a commercial supersonic transport aircraft."

Up to the end of 1966, the FAA had spent nearly $300 million in preliminary development of a feasible supersonic transport. The story of the supersonic transport—or SST, as it is called for short—is told in Chapter XIII. The huge aircraft is designed to carry more than 275 passengers over a distance of 4,000 miles at a speed of about 1,800 miles an hour. The eventual operation of this supersonic jet on commercial routes means that transatlantic flight time can be cut from seven to three hours, and the trip from Tokyo to Los Angeles via Honolulu need take only seven hours, meaning that Tokyo will be as close to Los Angeles, in terms of time, as Los Angeles was to New York during the final days of the piston-powered transports.

Each of the principal functions of the FAA, which have been outlined briefly above, will be discussed in subsequent chapters in greater detail, beginning with the most important FAA function of all—air traffic control.

V

Air Traffic Control

At more than 300 airports, both visual flight rule (VFR) and instrument flight rule (IFR) air traffic within a three- to thirty-mile radius is controlled from an FAA control tower. En route IFR air traffic flying along specified routes is controlled through FAA air route traffic control centers. Each tower and each center handles traffic within its own area, using radar and communications equipment to aid aircraft in navigating safely through the airspace it controls. As the flight progresses, control is transferred from center to center and, finally, from center to the airport control tower, if there is one at the destination landing field.

For the more than 300,000 general aviation pilots—those other than airline pilots who make up more than 95 per cent of all active civil aviation pilots—the FAA operates a third type of air traffic facility, the flight service station. Designed for use by military pilots as well as by civil pilots, approximately 400 of these flight service stations serve general aviation in the United States. They are usually located at airports where general aviation flying is heavy; each flight service station is responsible for an area of approximately 400 square miles. The FAA specialists who man the flight service stations are almost all experts on their particular area's terrain, on weather peculiarities, and on problems peculiar to their area. The flight service station specialists provide pilots with preflight and inflight weather information, suggested routes, altitudes, indications of turbulence, icing, and any other information important to the safety of a flight. When a general aviation airplane on a VFR flight plan fails to report within a reasonable period of time to its assigned station or at its destination, the flight service station orders a search and rescue operation.

Should the pilot become lost or have other problems, the flight service station provides orientation instructions as well as directions to the nearest suitable landing field. For aircraft flying under instrument flight rules, these emergency services are also available through the air route traffic control centers.

The FAA has been particularly active in helping airports served by the scheduled airlines to upgrade their instrument landing capabilities. As a rule, one runway, usually the longest, is equipped with special lighting as well as an instrument landing system (ILS). Radio aids include radio marker beacons, placed along the ground under the path of the ILS beam, which identify specific geographic points along the approach path.

A pilot utilizing the instrument landing system for a bad weather or poor visibility approach is guided by special radio beams to the threshold of the runway. At that point, the pilot changes from the instrument system to a visual approach. Minimum visibility requirements vary with the airport. If the pilot is able to see the ground from the minimum altitude and can see the required distance ahead, he is permitted to land.

The visibility minimums for what the FAA calls a Category I instrument landing condition are 200 feet of clear airspace above the runway and a forward visibility of half a mile. In the evolutionary effort to reduce airline schedule delays caused by weather, the FAA hopes eventually to have at least a limited number of key airports equipped for zero-zero visibility—Category III—instrument landings. In the meantime, a program is going forward to equip airports for Category II landings. These require a "decision height" visibility of 100 feet and forward visibility along the runway of at least 1,200 feet.

Ground equipment for Category II runway certification requires an improved instrument landing system, high-intensity approach lights, special lights in the touchdown zone (first 3,000 feet of runway), high-intensity runway edge lighting, centerline lights the full length of the runway and two "transmissometers," which measure visibility along the runway, one in the touchdown zone and one in the roll-out area.

The transmissometers measure the horizontal visibility in terms of runway visual range (RVR). The instrument is read on a dial in the airport control tower. The pilot coming in for a limited visibility landing is kept advised of the runway visual range at all times. If there is not sufficient visibility in the pilot's judgment so that he can adequately see the runway when he is 100 feet or more above it, or if the runway visual range drops below 1,200 feet, the rules require that the landing attempt be abandoned. The pilot then may either hold near the airport for an improvement in the weather or proceed to an alternate airport.

EN ROUTE TRAFFIC CONTROL

Between airports, pilots may proceed along established airways under visual flight rules (VFR) in good weather, or under instrument flight rules (IFR) if visibility is below minimums set by the FAA for safe visual flight. The airways, of course, are as invisible as the meridians of longitude or the parallels of latitude, and like meridians and parallels are shown on aeronautical charts in relation to the terrain beneath them. These charts, prepared by the Coast and Geodetic Survey, show rivers, lakes, highways, metropolitan areas, cities, towns, villages, mountains, cliffs, ridges, swamps, and marshes. Also clearly marked are the call signs, frequencies, and the location of navigation aids. These so-called navaids are radio transmission stations which provide identification and course information. Some also provide distance-from-the-station information.

The basic navigational aid is the VOR (very high-frequency omnidirectional radio range). Each VOR provides 360 separate radio course indications either to or from the transmitting station. The stations identify themselves to pilots either by three-letter Morse code signals or by a voice recording, sometimes by both. Almost 800 VOR stations are operating in the United States today. When a special radio receiver in the cockpit of the aircraft is tuned to the VOR station, the station will signal whether the particular course indication received is the one *to* the station or *away* from it. The pilot is then able to navigate cross-country by preselecting and following radials from various VOR stations along his planned route. He may also, by receiving bearing information from two VOR's, accurately determine his position by triangulation. The stations in many cases are also equipped to transmit weather information, generally twice each hour.

To make sure that all VOR stations operate within safe tolerances, they are continuously monitored by a fleet of aircraft that fly grid patterns back and forth across the United States. In addition to checking the VOR stations, these flying inspection laboratories check FAA's instrument landing systems, direction finders, marker beacons, and radio ranges, as well as the communication systems used between aircraft and control centers, control towers, and flight service stations.

GROWTH OF AIR TRAFFIC

Although once regarded as a limitless resource, the air-space of the United States by 1959 had become a heavily traveled network of skyways. Throughout the FAA's first year, air traffic problems continued to grow, not only because of the greater number of aircraft flying, but also because of the higher performance characteristics of the newer aircraft. According to the FAA annual report for 1960: "The expansion of air commerce, like that of our contemporary population, can best be characterized as 'explosive'. . . . Insuring the efficient utilization of this dwindling national resource ranks as one of the most important of the Agency's responsibilities."

During 1960, FAA air route traffic control centers handled nearly 10 million instrument flight movements along the 217,000 miles of designated federal airways. FAA control towers during 1960 logged nearly 26 million landings and take-offs, and its approach facilities guided nearly 1 million instrument approaches to airports. By the end of 1960, FAA was operating 646 air traffic control facilities, including 228 airport control towers, 339 flight service facilities stations, 35 air route traffic control centers, 34 military radar approach control centers, and 10 international air traffic communications stations.

On a typical day in 1960, there were more than 100,000 aircraft flights in operation across the nation. At the same time, FAA's capacity for providing instrument flight rule separation on a peak day was 22,500 flights. According to the agency, this and similar indices disclosed a gap between aviation's need for services and the government's capacity to serve. Because this gap had so widened in the period before effective federal machinery was created to try to solve the problem, it could not be closed immediately. In view of the anticipated growth and changing character of the services required, the agency predicted it would be sometime between 1963 and 1965, depending on many variable factors, before a reasonably adequate level of services could be obtained. In the meantime, in order to maintain safety standards, it was necessary at times to impose certain restrictions on air traffic flow.

One of the ways in which the problem of crowded airspace was met was the designation of certain airlanes as "positive control" routes—meaning that all aircraft operating along these routes at certain altitudes had to be under the direct control of an FAA air route traffic controller. The concept of positive control routes dated back to May, 1958, when the Civil Aeronautics Board adopted Special Civil Air Regulation 424, which authorized the CAA administrator to designate positive control route segments over any portion of the airspace between 17,000 and 35,000 feet, up to a width of 40 miles. Within this designated positive control zone, all visual flight rule (VFR) flights would be prohibited regardless of weather. Only instrument flight rule (IFR) operations conducted with the approval of FAA air traffic control would be permitted. This ruling represented a major modification of the Civil Aeronautics Authority's long established "see and be seen" philosophy, and took into account for the first time the extremely fast closing rates of high-performance aircraft.

On June 15, 1958, CAA acted under its new grant of authority and designated as positive control airways certain air route corridors which ran between the east and west coasts of the United States. CAA also designated as positive control routes certain supplemental and interconnecting route segments. Also at this time, the CAA adopted Greenwich Mean Time for all domestic air traffic control operations.

In September, 1959, FAA ordered an indefinite extension of these positive control regulations for the altitude between 17,000 and 22,000 feet on the three designated air routes or airways which link New York to Washington, D.C., on the four airways linking Los Angeles to San Francisco, and on the three airways between Washington and Chicago.

During 1961, the FAA took an important step forward in

the expansion of positive control in the airspace above 24,-000 feet, intending to complete procurement of positive control facilities and equipment by the fall of 1963. This would make positive control available throughout all forty-eight states, except for some areas of the extreme north central and northeastern sections of the country. By July 1, 1961, positive control was extended to more than 110,000 square miles of high-altitude airspace. Within the positive control area, all aircraft not only had to operate under instrument flight rules, regardless of the weather, but also had to be equipped with two-way radios for pilot-controller communication and a coded radar beacon transmitter for identification. These arrangements not only enhanced safety; the continuous radar monitoring also enabled FAA controllers to reduce the separation between aircraft. This more efficient use of the airspace was a beneficial by-product.

On September 17, 1964, the FAA revised its airway route structure to provide for two instead of three layers of traffic. Under the new system, short and intermediate range operations were combined in the area below 18,000 feet, while long-range operations were provided by a jet route structure between 18,000 and 45,000 feet. The airspace above 45,000 feet was designated for point-to-point operations on a random routing basis. The old three-layer scheme provided for a low-altitude airways up to 14,500 feet, an intermediate airways system between 14,500 and 24,000 feet, and jet routes above 24,000 feet. FAA's 1964 annual report to Congress pointed out that the revised air route structure was "designed to profit from experience provided by operations in a high-altitude portion of the 1961 layout. Experience has proved that for such operations the workload on both pilot and controller is reduced; the need to consult charts in the cockpit is less frequent, and there are fewer radio contacts to be made and fewer navigational check points."

RADAR

Next to the high-frequency radio telephone, radar is the basic tool used by the FAA to monitor and control air traffic. Essentially, a radar transmitter is like a searchlight which sends out beams of energy. An airplane in the path of this beam of energy reflects some of it back to the ground, where it is picked up by a receiving antenna. This reflected energy is amplified to produce a bright spot on a radar scope. FAA radar antennas do two things: first, they rotate throughout 360 degrees of arc, and, second, they combine the receiving element with the transmitting antenna. This enables the FAA not only to determine the direction of the energy return but also, by calibration of the time it takes for the energy pulse to travel from the radar transmitter to the airplane and to be reflected back and received, to determine how far the target echo is from the radar site. Thus the air traffic controller has a visual display before him which gives roughly the position and distance of any airborne object (the "target") which reflects energy back from the radar beam. This basic radar surveillance system is called primary radar and has been used for air traffic control by the FAA since 1952. Many improvements have been made in the radar system since the FAA first began using this electronic aid, developed during World War II. Bright-display radar, which makes it possible for controllers to work in a normally lighted room and still see the radar displays and the targets with their glowing blips, is one important improvement.

One problem that has not been fully solved results from the fact that the radar scope display is two-dimensional. Since the entire vertical column of airspace is simultaneously scanned by the radar, targets may appear to collide on the scope when, in fact, they may be several thousand feet apart in altitude. Another problem which radar does not solve is identification of target. Nearly all military and air carriers by

1964 had standard 64-code identification (SIF) equipment but were not capable of reporting altitude. The usual way to identify a target is to contact the aircraft by radio and ask the pilot to make a certain sequence of turns. These can then be picked out on the radar scope because of the distinctive movement of the target blip. With the target thus identified, altitude can be obtained from the pilot by voice radio. Such a system is, however, both cumbersome and time-consuming. In an effort to overcome these defects, FAA scientists developed the system widely referred to as the air traffic control radar beacon system (ATCRBS). In this system, an addition to the radar makes it possible for a separate "interrogation" pulse of energy to be sent out on command from the rotating antenna. When the aircraft receives this interrogation pulse, a beacon in the airplane answers with another signal, which is received on the ground. In order for this system to operate, the airplane, on command, must be able to flash a signal which gives both its identification number and its altitude. By early 1964, all FAA en route traffic control centers were equipped with radar beacon interrogation equipment, and most high-traffic-density terminal area control towers also had such equipment. By then, all airline jet aircraft were also equipped with radar beacon identity transponders, as were most airline turboprop aircraft. By FAA rule, airborne radar beacon equipment is required for all aircraft operating above 24,000 feet.

By mid-1966, FAA planned to add equipment on the ground to make a so-called alpha-numeric display of altitude and identification possible whenever traffic demands justify the expense. As envisioned, the system will make it possible for the reply pulse from the aircraft to be converted into a series of numbers electronically. Ever since radar was first used for air traffic control, these numbers have had to be marked by hand on plastic markers called "shrimp boats," which are then placed on the scope near the aircraft targets.

The shrimp boats are moved manually as the targets move. Eventually a computer will display the numbers on the radar scope and will automatically move the numbers along with the target.

FAA FACILITIES

During fiscal year 1965, FAA decommissioned a number of its obsolete facilities. Twenty-one low-frequency radio ranges were phased out, and several of the sixty remaining low-frequency ranges were scheduled for conversion to non-directional radio beacons, with the balance scheduled to be decommissioned. Five intermediate landing fields—remainders of the early airmail route system—were transferred to the local sponsors who were operating them as public airports. Only one intermediate landing field continues in operation in the United States. This installation, located at Hanksville, Utah, has been retained for emergency purposes, as well as to provide logistic support to FAA facilities located in that remote area. During fiscal year 1965, 143 airway light beacons were discontinued; these, too, were highly useful during the early airmail route days when even night flights operated by reference to ground landmarks.

On the other hand, the placing of identification signs on the top of buildings to guide lost airmen is an active FAA program even today. The head of the FAA's air-marking branch is a veteran woman pilot, Mrs. Blanche W. Noyes. An employee of FAA and its predecessor agencies since 1936, Mrs. Noyes is in charge of all federal air-marking programs for the United States and its territories. In addition, Mrs. Noyes has helped many foreign countries, including Brazil, which awarded her a silver medal of merit in 1966 for setting up air-marking systems tailored to the specific needs of that country.

FAA's air navigation facilities are often located in out-of-the-way places. Special access roads must sometimes be built to install the facilities in the first place, and the roads then must be maintained to provide continued access for maintenance. During 1963, one such road was under construction on Mount Kaala, the highest peak on Oahu Island, in Hawaii, on top of which a long-range radar was being installed. In nine western states, the FAA maintains more than 1,000 miles of roads that have no reason for existence other than to provide access to FAA facilities. These roads are sometimes hazardous, and the death of at least one FAA maintenance employee has been attributed to a road hazard accident. During winter, special snow vehicles are used in maintenance. Ski tows and even helicopters help to keep some facilities in operation.

At Juneau, Alaska, the difficult terrain surrounding the airport requires a special navigation aid, unique in the civil-military system. The range of mountains that rings the airport prevents the use of standard airport approach devices, such as the instrument landing system (ILS). At the same time, weather conditions frequently make instrument approaches necessary. The solution is a Localizer Type Directional Approach Aid, which, because Juneau can be reached only by water or air, has done much to alleviate a serious economic condition there. Other types of special navigation aids have had to be installed at Marquette, Michigan, at La Guardia Airport in New York City, and at Deer Park Airport, New York.

Flight operations throughout the national airspace system during 1965 exceeded that of any previous year. At the end of the year, FAA was operating 292 airport traffic control towers, an increase of 14 over the previous year. These towers handled a record 37.9 million take-offs and landings during the year—an 11 per cent increase over 1964. Nearly one-fourth of all airport operations were conducted under instrument flight rules (IFR), an increase of 15 per cent. The biggest increase in IFR traffic was by general aviation, which showed a jump of 34 per cent in instrument flight operations in 1965, whereas airline instrument flight activity increased by only 14 per cent.

The one-millionth aircraft monitored by the New York air route traffic control center in 1965 was an Eastern Airlines Boeing 727 jet which reported into Islip, Long Island, on December 28 while en route from Newark to Miami. The flight established a record, not only for the FAA facility but for the world. The previous record, also held by the Islip center, was 892,384 flight movements during 1964.

In considering traffic growth, it is interesting to note that general aviation has been training pilots to higher qualifications, and the use of aircraft equipped for instrument flight has expanded in recent years to the point where general aviation constituted almost 30 per cent of FAA's instrument flight rule load in 1966. The Aircraft Owners and Pilots Association has predicted that by 1980 general aviation could very well constitute 70 per cent of the load and the air carriers share could decline to 30 percent—a complete reversal of the present situation.

IMPROVEMENTS IN AIR TRAFFIC CONTROL

How did it all start? The first control tower to use radio to handle airport traffic was established in 1930 at the Cleveland, Ohio, Municipal Airport. By 1935, approximately twenty cities had followed Cleveland's lead and were operating municipal airport radio control towers. Then in December, 1935, the first airway traffic control center was set up at Newark, New Jersey. The center was organized, manned, and supported by the airline companies. Its purpose was to supply information to airline pilots on the whereabouts of other planes in the Newark vicinity when it was necessary to operate under marginal weather conditions. In 1936, two additional centers were organized and staffed for the Chicago and Cleveland terminal areas. Later in the year, all three were taken over by the Bureau of Air Commerce. On May 24, 1946, the first radar-equipped control center for civilian flying was established at the Indianapolis Airport by the CAA, using the basic radar system developed for the armed forces, with certain improvements added by CAA's industrial engineers.

This is looking at air traffic from the viewpoint of the FAA controller. From the pilot's viewpoint, the most important navigation aid available to him is the nearest VOR station. Utilizing very high-frequency radio beams, the pilot, if his aircraft is suitably equipped with a receiver, can not only determine the VOR station's heading from his position, but also fly down the selected radial beam to a point directly over the VOR station. At this point, the beam will carry him outward on the same heading until he abandons the weakening signal behind him for a fresh signal ahead. If he is also equipped with distance measuring equipment (DME), the counter on his dial will tell him, mile by mile, how far he is from the VOR station to which he is tuned. He thus is able to know his exact position at all times.

VOR is being improved. During 1965, the FAA tested a new method of producing VOR signals which would be compatible with, and from five to ten times more accurate than, signals from standard equipment now in use. Development of DME ground stations suitable for en route and terminal use, both at home and abroad, was also completed during 1965, fulfilling a promise made to the International Civil Aviation Organization in 1958. To help establish the worldwide VOR/DME navigation system adopted by that organization, the FAA, working with the Department of State, took steps to loan DME equipment to twelve foreign countries for installation at key points on international air routes. The agency had already equipped sixty VOR facilities with identification by voice as well as Morse code, and had installed greatly improved all-band VOR antenna systems on approximately 150 high-frequency navigational aids.

The FAA has not neglected the airport control towers in its modernization efforts. Administrator Halaby, for example, wanted the FAA to make airports more attractive. This led to a standardized air traffic control tower designed by I. M. Pei, the outstanding American architect who designed the John F. Kennedy Library at Harvard University. On the recommendation of a top level advisory committee, Mr. Pei was commissioned to design a standard control tower that would be both functional and attractive. The design was widely praised, and Halaby hoped that Mr. Pei's tower would be used all over the United States, perhaps even around the world.

Unfortunately, when the FAA supplied funds to community airports to build these attractive control tower buildings, the General Accounting Office, so-called watchdog of the treasury, objected, claiming in a special report to Congress that the Pei design stressed aesthetic factors at the expense of cost. The new towers, which were not only more attractive, but more useful, cost about $80,000 more than the old-style cracker-box towers. The General Accounting Office's criticism was not echoed in Congress, or anywhere else, but Administrator McKee, Halaby's successor, ordered the FAA to abandon the Pei design.

Improvement in the traffic control system is never-ending. Between 1958 and 1965, the FAA increased by more than 50 per cent the number of facilities making up the nation's air traffic control and navigation system, representing a national investment of $1.25 billion. The system cost about half a billion dollars annually to operate and maintain, but by 1965 it had no equal throughout the world for safety and efficiency.

VI

Air Safety Problems—
Human and Legal

Problems of safe flight have concerned airmen since the beginning of flying. The Wright brothers were safety conscious from the start. Their bicycle manufacturing business at Dayton, Ohio, was based on a so-called safety bicycle design, which made use of smaller wheels than the huge high-wheelers that had formerly been popular. When they began experimenting with gliders in the Kill Devil Hills area of the North Carolina coast, they were quite cautious, particularly at the start of their experiments. In the course of their 1901–02 gliding experiments, they made more than a thousand short gliding flights, not only to develop efficient methods of control, but also for the purpose of teaching themselves instinctively to control their gliding machines.

In a paper delivered before the Western Society of Engineers in Chicago on June 24, 1903, Wilbur Wright described some of these experimental glides. After reporting that the method of controlling their gliders was different from that used by most other experimenters, who shifted their weight about to effect balance, Wilbur Wright confessed that the Wright gliders had reached "a higher state of development than the operators," who, even after much practice, were "little more than novices" in the management of their aircraft. "A thousand glides is equivalent to about four hours of steady practice, far too little to give anyone a complete mastery of the art of flying." Wilbur wrote. "Before trying to rise to any dangerous height a man ought to know that in an emergency his mind and muscles will work by instinct rather than by conscious effort. There is no time to think."

In general, the gliding experiments of the Wright brothers were free of accidents, except for hard landings when the wind suddenly died down. One such hard landing, which resulted in more than minor damage to the glider, was described by Wilbur Wright in the paper mentioned above. Orville was at the controls and Wilbur observed that, after a few preliminary flights to accustom himself to a new method of operating the front "rudder" (or elevator, as it would be called today), Orville felt ready to undertake the management of the lateral, wing-warping control also. Shortly after beginning to glide, he found himself with one wing slightly higher than the other. This caused the machine to swing to the left. After waiting a moment to see whether the plane would right itself, Orville applied warping control to the wings to straighten the aircraft out. At the very moment that he did this, the right wing rose even higher, and Orville had a moment of confusion when he tried to determine whether it was his applying control that had made the wing rise or whether this was something unrelated to the control movement. After a moment's thought, Orville decided that he had made the right control movement and increased it. In the meantime, he had neglected the front rudder, which maintained fore and aft balance. As a consequence, the machine turned its nose up higher and higher until it assumed what Wilbur called a most dangerous attitude. "We who were on the ground," wrote Wilbur, "noticed this in advance of the aviator, who was thoroughly absorbed in the attempt to restore the lateral balance, but our shouts of alarm were drowned by the howling of the wind. It was only when the machine came to a stop and started backwards that he at length realized the true situation." From a height of about thirty feet, Orville found himself sailing diagonally backwards until he struck the ground. He had only time for one hasty glance behind him before he found himself tangled in the wreckage of his glider. "How he escaped injury I do not know," Wilbur concluded, "but afterwards he was unable to show a scratch or bruise anywhere, though his clothes were torn in one place."

According to Wilbur, this was an unusual accident because of the height to which the aircraft ascended. Even though Orville's maximum altitude before this accident was not much more than three times, or at most four times, the height of a man, it was much higher than the Wrights usually glided. Normally they kept the aircraft low, skimming the ground at heights of only a few inches at times. From the beginning, the Wrights avoided unnecessary risks. Higher flights were more spectacular, they knew, but the lower ones were just as valuable for practice purposes. "Skill comes by the constant repetition of familiar feats rather than by a few overbold attempts at feats for which the performer is yet poorly prepared," wrote Wilbur.

After their extensive experiments with gliders, the Wright brothers built a power machine with two propellers, driven from a single engine, and with this machine made the world's first successful heavier-than-air flights on December 17, 1903. But it was many years and many flights later before the Wright brothers were ready to demonstrate to a skeptical public what they had accomplished.

In the summer of 1908, Wilbur Wright took one plane to France in an attempt to interest the French government in purchasing the aircraft. On Saturday, August 8, Wilbur took off from a racetrack near Le Mans, France. He flew for less than two minutes. The following Monday he made two short flights, during which he performed banked turns and a figure eight, thus confounding the critics who had called the Wright brothers *bluffeurs*.

While the crowned heads of Europe were flocking to France to see Wilbur fly, Orville was putting another Wright machine through the U.S. Army acceptance tests at Fort Myers, across the Potomac River from Washington, D.C. On September 9, Orville astonished the world by flying forty miles in one hour and two minutes, thus being the first man ever to fly for more than one hour in a heavier-than-air craft. Orville later made flights of more than an hour almost daily, and on September 9 took up his first passenger for a six-minute flight. On September 17, Orville took up another passenger and met with his first serious accident. It was also the first serious accident ever suffered by a heavier-than-air craft. During the flight, a crack developed in one of the propellers, setting up a vibration that resulted, indirectly, in the snapping of a stay wire connected to the vertical stabilizers in the tail. The machine crashed, and Orville's passenger, Army Lieutenant Thomas Selfridge, was killed—the world's first aircraft passenger fatality. Orville himself broke several bones and was badly bruised.

Although the Wright planes were probably the safest in the air in those early days of flying, many exhibition flyers lost their lives in Wright planes, mainly through stunting. If there had been an FAA in those days, the Wright airplanes might have been certificated in the "normal" category, but even slow spins would have been prohibited.

Is the FAA Too Rules-Minded?

How would the Wright brothers feel about FAA if they were flying today? No one knows, of course, but some pilots —particularly those who fly for pleasure and the sheer personal satisfaction of flying—believe that the Federal Aviation Administration is too rules-minded and that it depends

Left to right: FAA administrators Charles F. Horne, Delos W. Rentzel, and Elwood R. Quesada and former CAA administrators Donald W. Nyrop, Frederick B. Lee, Najeeb E. Halaby, William F. McKee, and Theodore P. Wright on the rooftop helipad of the FAA building, Washington, D.C.

Night view of Dulles International Airport.

Federal Aviation Agency

One of FAA's fleet of mobile lounges used to transport passengers between planes and the Dulles Airport terminal.

Aerial view of Dulles International Airport.

Runway 36, Washington National Airport. The high-intensity lighting is used for poor-visibility landings.

Inside the control tower, Washington National Airport. On the runway is one of the "short haul" jets that have drawn criticism for their high noise level on take-off and landing.

Control tower at Dulles International Airport.

Three flight-check aircraft equipped as laboratories to test the strength and accuracy of FAA's 4,000 navigational aids at various altitudes.

Very high-frequency omnidirectional radio range (VOR) transmitter.

Instrument landing system transmitter building and antenna.

Federal Aviation Agency

An FAA flight inspector shows a student pilot the maneuvers he will be expected to perform for his flight test.

Interior of an FAA multi-engine jet flying laboratory.

Lieutenant Selfridge (left) and Orville Wright before taking off on the fatal flight of September 17, 1908.

After the crash. Orville Wright survived, but Lieutenant Selfridge died a few hours later of a head injury.

Comforting the dying Selfridge, the first air passenger fatality.

An FAA crash test. Out of such tests come valuable data for changes in safety rules.

Interior of test plane. Both forward and rearward seating was tested, but results were not sufficiently conclusive to require a change from the present forward seating used by the airlines.

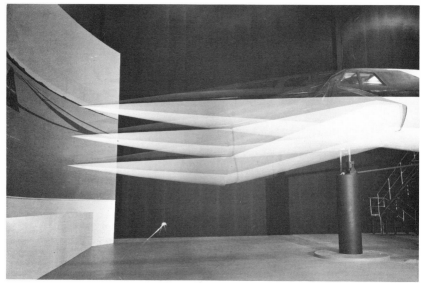

Triple-exposure photograph showing positions of the Boeing supersonic's movable nose.

Multiple-exposure photograph of the Boeing supersonic's variable-sweep wing.

too much on federal air regulations to advance the cause of air safety. FAA's first administrator didn't agree. In March, 1959, Administrator Quesada urged all of FAA's regional administrators, regional attorneys, and key flight standards personnel to use FAA's new rule-making powers to the fullest in the interest of air safety. Enforcement activities, he said, should be "firm, fair, fast, and factual."

During its first year, the FAA issued over 400 new safety rules and regulations. These covered such subjects as airborne weather radar, instrument proficiency of pilots, approved flight recorders for transport aircraft, copilot proficiency, oxygen mask requirements, and airmen training programs.

All transport category aircraft, with certain very limited exceptions, were required by a 1960 order to carry weather radar equipment. In another rule covering airmen proficiency levels, the FAA said that applicants for both private and commercial pilot ratings must demonstrate a degree of knowledge and skill in the use of instrument flying. To aid in the determination of accident causes, the FAA required that flight recorders—mechanical devices which automatically record air speed, altitude, time, vertical acceleration, and heading—be installed on all turbine-powered airplanes of more than 12,500 pounds used in air carrier operations. Copilots on air carrier aircraft, according to another rule issued in 1960, must possess adequate knowledge and skill to fly safely to its destination the particular aircraft to which they are assigned.

Late in December, 1961, the FAA put into effect the first nation-wide air traffic rule for flight operations in and around controlled airports. New rules included a speed limit of 250 knots (288 miles per hour) for aircraft operating below 10,000 feet within 30 miles of the destination airport. The new rules, effective at all airports with federal control tower service, covered airport traffic areas, approach and departure procedures, and pattern altitudes, and required a two-way radio communication system on all aircraft using airports with active control towers.

In its report to Congress for 1960, the FAA emphasized that "the basic objective of enforcement is compliance. It is a means by which FAA seeks to convert safety standards from a concept to reality. It serves to protect the many conscientious pilots from the irresponsible few, and to provide the safest possible flying environment for all airspace users." During 1960, the agency processed 5,000 reports of violations and took action on 4,000 cases. Of 3,000 completed enforcement actions, about 1,000 involved certificate action against airmen, air carriers, and air agencies. Approximately 12 per cent of all such certificate action cases were appealed by the holder to the Civil Aeronautics Board. The total dollar amount of civil penalties that were compromised and paid was 150 per cent of the 1959 total. In addition, two formal investigations of air carrier type operations resulted in the agency's refusal to reissue a commercial operator certificate. Of violations involving military personnel during 1960, 136 cases were referred to the Department of Defense for corrective or disciplinary action.

The Federal Aviation Act of 1958 transferred from the Civil Aeronautics Board to the FAA the responsibility for issuing safety rules and regulations. Since the establishment of FAA coincided with the major airline transition to jet transport aircraft, the agency in its first year issued a number of new rules and regulations covering performance and operation of the new jet transports. Among the most important safety decisions of the year was a new Civil Air Regulation prohibiting any pilot over sixty years of age from participating in air carrier flight operations. Another safety measure required that air carrier training programs for flight crew members be approved by FAA. Initial training and proficiency tests were made more detailed for all copilots and pilots serving as second in command of commercial airliners. The FAA during the year also studied the effectiveness of various oxygen systems at high altitudes and investigated sudden illnesses that might possibly incapacitate flight crews.

Also during 1959, the FAA ordered its flight inspectors to enforce a requirement that flight crew members on commercial transports remain at their duty stations during flight. The enforcement crackdown came after a near-tragic accident involving a transatlantic jet airliner with 119 passengers aboard, which went out of control when its autopilot became disengaged. The copilot was filling out reports at the time, and the captain was in the passenger cabin. The plane dived nearly 25,000 feet before it was brought under control by its crew. During the same year, the FAA amended the Civil Air Regulations to prohibit the operation of an aircraft by anyone whose medical background included: (1) an established diagnosis of diabetes requiring treatment with insulin; (2) a history of myocardial infarction or other evidence of coronary arterial disease; (3) an established diagnosis of psychosis, severe psychoneurosis, or severe personality difficulties; or (4) an established diagnosis of epilepsy, alcoholism, or drug addiction.

Tough rule-making and enforcement policies were probably needed to shake up the aviation community and make it more aware of the need for a greater respect for air safety rules. At the same time, the new agency's actions drew much criticism from those who felt that enforcement of the rules was too arbitrary. As a result, when Administrator Halaby took over, one of the first things he did was to appoint a group of consultants to examine FAA's rule-making and enforcement procedures. This study, known as Project Tightrope, was headed by Lloyd N. Cutler of Washington, D.C. The study group, composed of prominent attorneys experienced in administrative law and aviation problems, made a number of important recommendations, which resulted in changes of procedures. The positions of chief hearing officer and hearing officer were established in the office of the administrator of FAA in January, 1962, as a result. These positions provided airmen with a trial-type proceeding, in which they could plead their cases when charged with a violation of the Federal Air Regulations that might result in suspension or revocation of their certificates. A hearing by an FAA hearing officer would not in any way prevent the airman from exercising his statutory right to appeal an FAA decision to the Civil Aeronautics Board. Such appeals are now handled by the Transportation Safety Board under the Transportation Act of 1966.

PIRACY, SABOTAGE, AND TAPE RECORDERS

During 1962, two aspects of aviation safety made headlines: hijacking and other crimes aboard aircraft in flight, and the problem of insane passengers who smuggle explosives aboard aircraft in order to destroy the plane—and sometimes themselves—in the air.

Hijacking made front-page news in May, 1961, when a passenger on a flight from Miami to Key West hijacked the aircraft and forced the pilot to divert to Havana. Cuban authorities permitted the plane and passengers—minus the hijacker—to return to Miami. Later that year, a drunken passenger, who boarded a nonstop flight from Chicago to Los Angeles, became angry when he was forced to give up a private supply of liquor and attacked the pilot with a knife. After the plane landed, the offender escaped prosecution because of a conflict of jurisdiction. In order to plug this gap in the criminal code, the late Senator Clair Engle of California introduced a bill in the Senate to amend the Federal Aviation Act of 1958 to make it a federal offense to commit assaults and certain other crimes of violence aboard aircraft in flight. In the House, Representative John Bell Williams of

Mississippi introduced a similar bill, which, after various amendments, became Public Law 87-197, an Act "to amend the Federal Aviation Act of 1958 to provide for the application of federal criminal law to certain events occurring aboard aircraft in air commerce." The Act was signed by President John Kennedy on September 5, 1961.

Before the law was passed, there had been several more incidents. On July 25, a supporter of Cuba's Premier Fidel Castro forced a U.S. passenger plane to deviate from a flight over Florida and land in Havana. Cuban authorities allowed the passengers and crew to return to Miami but did not release the plane for several weeks. On August 2, two American citizens attempted to force a passenger plane on a flight from Phoenix to Houston to go to Cuba; however, the captain landed the plane at El Paso, Texas, giving as his reason the need for refueling. Although the highjackers held the crew and some of the passengers captive for several hours, the two men were finally overpowered. In a third incident during the summer of 1961, a French Algerian forced a U.S. plane in flight over Mexico to proceed to Havana, but the Cuban authorities kept only the highjacker and permitted the plane and all the passengers to go on to Miami.

The law signed by President Kennedy in September, 1961, provided for death or imprisonment of not less than twenty years for the crime of aircraft piracy, defined as "any seizure or exercise of control, by force or violence or threat of force or violence, and with wrongful intent, of an aircraft in flight and air commerce." The new law also provided punishment for interference with flight crew members or flight attendants in the performance of their duties. In addition, the law made provisions for applying pertinent parts of the U.S. Code to certain crimes committed aboard aircraft in flight. Only a duly authorized person might carry a concealed weapon aboard an air carrier engaged in air commerce. Punishment was also provided for giving false information concerning an attempt, or even an alleged attempt, to perpetrate any of the crimes covered by the provisions of the Act. The Act also authorized air carriers, under such rules as the FAA might provide, to refuse transportation to any passenger or to any property when, in the air carrier's opinion, such transportation might be dangerous to flight safety. To help enforce the new law, the FAA established a special corps of safety inspectors, who were trained for emergency duty as peace officers aboard airline flights. All of the men were graduates of the special course of instruction given at the U.S. Border Patrol Academy.

One problem which has not yet been solved, despite many efforts, is how to detect in advance a mentally disturbed person—or the bomb that he plans to explode aboard an aircraft. On May 22, 1962, an airliner on a regularly scheduled flight from Chicago to Kansas City blew up over Iowa, killing thirty-seven passengers and a crew of eight. A federal investigation determined that the tragedy resulted from a dynamite explosion aboard the plane. Since legislation covering the bombing of aircraft was enacted as early as 1956, there was no question that the action was illegal.

During fiscal 1962, FAA spent about $47,000 in an effort to find a solution to this problem. During 1963 and 1964, this sum was increased to $125,000. Investigations are still going on into the feasibility of using X-rays, fluoroscopes, moisture analysis, microwaves, chemical techniques, even biological techniques for detecting bombs. One project considered was begun by the Atomic Energy Commission during 1960 at the request of FAA Administrator Quesada. It involved the "seeding" of all commercially manufactured explosives with an atomic tracer isotope that can be easily detected by special instruments.

Since the first known incident occurred in 1933, there have been eighteen sabotage incidents throughout the world. In the years 1955–65, sabotage accidents took place at the rate of one or two per year; six fatal accidents of this type occurred in the United States during these ten years. A total of 210 persons—27 crew members and 183 passengers—lost their lives in these accidents.

The Air Line Pilots Association established a standing committee for the study of sabotage problems. This committee has stated that "one clear and indisputable conclusion has stood out in these studies: financial gain has figured consistently and prominently in aircraft sabotage; insurance has been so far the most prevalent, if not the only common denominator; and the predominant insurance vehicle used has been airport vended insurance." The committee cited two examples. One was the case of a dutiful son who put his mother aboard a United Air Lines DC-6, her baggage containing a bomb that caused a mid-air explosion killing forty-four people, in order to collect the insurance on her life, purchased from an airport vending machine. The other was that of a West Coast businessman who, after losing heavily during a gambling spree, took out a $105,000 life insurance policy before boarding his flight home. While the plane was over Danville, California, he shot the pilot; the subsequent crash caused the death of forty-four persons. The Air Line Pilots Association has been unable to persuade the FAA or the Civil Aeronautics Board that making it difficult for would-be suicides or murderers to buy flight insurance easily and cheaply would cause the incidence of sabotage to decline. In 1966, however, the association was successful in having several bills introduced in Congress to limit the sale of machine-vended and over-the-counter trip insurance to a maximum liability of $50,000. In commenting on this legislation, the association claimed that

> commercial interests that profit from this type of insurance won't voluntarily do what is necessary because the steady flow of quarters mounts up to exceedingly big money. In some instances, the airport gets as much as 17 cents; the "take" at

some larger airports running into the multi-hundreds of thousands of dollars a year. If adequate safeguards are to be provided the public against this "lottery in lives," it is obvious they must come from congressional action.

One of the most valuable accident investigation tools available to investigators is the metal tape recorder, which can be recovered after a crash and "read out" to determine just what the plane was doing during the period immediately preceding the accident. Early in 1966, the FAA announced several changes in its flight recorder rules that would provide better protection for recorders during a crash, make them easier to find afterward, and improve their accuracy. Flight recorders are now installed as far back in the airplane as practical to minimize the possibility of container rupture from crash impact. The rearward location also provides better protection from fire.

As early as 1948, the Civil Aeronautics Authority required air carrier and commercial aircraft operators to carry flight recorders on all large transport aircraft. Since 1960, the FAA has required flight recorders on all turbine-powered aircraft without regard to altitude of operation. The flight recorders are connected to the engine and aircraft performance instruments so that a continuous record is kept of the aircraft's bearing, altitude, air speed, and vertical acceleration (gravity forces). The data are recorded in intervals of seconds and fractions of seconds. Each bit of information traces a line on a metal foil, which feeds slowly through the recorder during the flight.

Until 1966, there were no specific rules covering the installation of recorders. They were frequently installed in locations that did not provide protection from crash impact forces. New rules now require that recorders be colored either bright orange or yellow to make them easier to find if they are thrown clear of the aircraft. The new rules also require operators to conduct and retain periodic accuracy tests to prove the correlation between the flight recorder readings and the visual readings of the plane's instruments, so that they can be consulted later, if needed, during a crash investigation. The FAA also requires that the recorder be capable of withstanding submersion in sea water for thirty-six hours. Impact tests call for dropping a 500-pound steel bar on the recorder from a height of ten feet. Fire-resistance tests require exposing the recorder to flames of 1,100 degrees centigrade. The test for static crash resistance calls for the application of a force of 5,000 pounds continuously for five minutes to each of the container's sides. To supplement the information available from the instrument recorders, the FAA in 1965 ordered the installation and use of cockpit voice recorders in large transport airplanes operated by air carriers and commercial operators.

NEW RULES AND REGULATIONS

Until the establishment of the Federal Aviation Agency in 1958, there was no codified federal air regulation system. The body of regulations built up over the years by the Civil Aeronautics Authority had been rather haphazardly issued and did not follow any particular form or order. One of the first decisions made by the FAA was to organize the regulations so as to eliminate duplications and overlapping definitions. This was the job of James B. Minor, then FAA associate general counsel and head of the general counsel's Regulations and Codifications Division. It was Mr. Minor's job to write new regulations and keep track of the old ones, taking old and disused Federal Air Regulations off the book.

At one time there was a Civil Air Regulation which spelled out the qualifications and duties of aircraft radio operators. This radio specialist job was gradually phased out of aviation when communications became almost entirely voice, and Morse code was all but abandoned. Even the navigation aids that once were identified by Morse code signals are today often equipped for voice identification. As a result, it is the job of the pilot or the copilot in most aircraft to handle communications, and the Federal Aviation Administration no longer issues an aircraft radio operators license.

When the Civil Air Regulations were codified into the new Federal Air Regulations shortly after the FAA was established, Minor recommended that an organized follow-up program be undertaken to review the contents of the Federal Air Regulations to determine if they serve the needs of present-day airmen and, if not, whether they should be modified or even dropped. For budget reasons this has not yet been done. The codification program reduced the number of regulations by more than three-quarters—a major step forward in the simplification of the regulations.

Minor is a lawyer with long government experience and an enthusiastic private pilot. It is his basic job to take the memoranda flowing in from the various operating arms of the agency and translate requests for federal air regulations into proper legal language. After the proposed regulation is drafted, it goes to the top-level Regulatory Council, which studies the draft and the need for the proposed regulation. Without the endorsement of the Regulatory Council, the draft is not made public. If the council approves, the proposed regulation is published in the government's official daily gazette, *The Federal Register*. In almost all cases, publication is in the form of a tentative proposal, and comments are invited. On the basis of these comments, the regulation may be modified, withdrawn, or issued. Almost all are modified as a result of the comments received.

One example of the agency's work in proposing new regulations was the effort made early in 1967 to alter the requirements for private pilot licenses so that pilots with limited experience could get greater enjoyment from flying while improving their skills. The proposed changes were the result

of several years of study and cooperation with various segments of the general aviation industry. The studies began
with an examination of the actual work done by a private
pilot in one of today's light airplanes. Workload was computed, and the level of skills necessary to perform each flying
task was analyzed.

This led to the conclusion that relatively simple skills were
needed to fly relatively simple aircraft. On the other hand, a
pilot who undertook to fly a sophisticated plane, even
though it might be powered by a single engine, would find
his task much more difficult, and he would need a substantially higher level of skill and experience. Under previous
FAA requirements, a private pilot had to pass a comprehensive written examination which covered all phases of flight.
In addition, he was required to pass a complex practical test,
including the demonstration of his ability to handle the aircraft while operating solely on instruments. The written
examination for private pilots was almost the same as that for
commercial pilots.

Under the proposed regulations published in *The Federal
Register* on January 9, 1967, the new "basic pilot" certificate,
which could be obtained without a written examination,
would require less training and experience. It could be issued
on endorsement of an FAA-licensed instructor and would
allow the basic pilot to carry passengers when operating relatively simple types of planes, such as those with nonretract-
able landing gear, fixed instead of variable-pitched propellers, no flaps, and a minimum stalling speed of sixty miles
per hour or less. Pilots with basic pilot ratings would be
limited to flight during daylight hours, when cloud ceilings
were at least 1,000 feet above the ground, and visibility was
at least five miles. Basic pilots would not be allowed to operate aircraft for hire or for compensation. Pilots holding the
basic certificate would, however, be permitted to operate
more sophisticated planes, without passengers, if they were

checked out and certified in that type of airplane by an FAA-licensed flight instructor. Except for five hours of cross-country solo flying, no minimum amount of flight time would be required for a basic pilot certificate. Responsibility for licensing would rest with the pilot's flight instructor, who would determine for himself when the student had attained sufficient competence in flight maneuvers and other skills. It was expected that about thirty-five hours of flight training and experience would be sufficient to qualify most applicants for the basic pilot certificate. To obtain a private pilot certificate, the requirements for flight training and experience would be changed to include more airborne training under the supervision of FAA-licensed flight instructors. This upgrading of private pilot requirements was expected to make a private pilot eligible for an instrument rating with no additional flight time. Previous regulations required private pilots to have at least 200 flight hours before they could apply for an instrument rating.

The same proposed regulations would upgrade commercial pilot certificates by requiring 250 hours of flight experience, 50 hours more than was previously required. In addition, an instrument rating would be required for the commercial license. Under the present rules only limited instrument training is required.

In announcing the proposed new regulations, the FAA claimed that existing regulations were based on the characteristics of airplanes developed more than a decade ago, and that raising private and commercial pilot requirements was necessary to bring piloting skills and techniques up to a level more nearly commensurate with the demands of today's more complex, high-performance planes.

THE ALCOHOL PROBLEM

The problem of pilots who drink before flying is confined almost entirely to pilots in general aviation. On July 8, 1965, the FAA proposed a new and tighter regulation covering drinking before flying. In support of the proposed regulation, FAA announced that "medical examinations performed on 158 pilots killed in general aviation aircraft accidents during 1963 disclosed measurable traces of alcohol in 56 cases. In 1964 alcohol was found in 78 out of 193 pilot accident fatalities examined, an increase of 6 per cent over 1963. In about 10 per cent of the 78 cases, alcohol levels of the blood were so high as to indicate advanced drunkenness."

The only regulation then in effect was an FAA rule which prohibited any person from operating an aircraft while "under the influence of intoxicating liquor." In place of this, the FAA proposed substituting an amendment to Part 91 of the Federal Aviation Regulations, which would prohibit any person from acting as a crew member of a civil aircraft within eight hours after he had consumed any alcoholic beverage. FAA pointed out that, while commercial carriers carefully regulate drinking habits of their air crews and usually enforce a twenty-four-hour abstinence before flight, no general rule prevailed among other pilots. Many private and business pilots did not seem aware that ability to operate an aircraft remains impaired many hours after drinking—even after the alcohol has left the bloodstream. FAA also pointed out that altitude has a marked effect on a pilot who has been drinking. At 10,000 feet, for example, the physiological effect of alcohol is twice as great as at sea level.

This rule-making proposal drew considerable comment from public and press. A majority of the comments favored the agency's objectives. However, some spokesmen for industry opposed the regulation on the grounds that it would be unenforceable, and that present rules and regulations were sufficient to cover all exigencies. Others said that the proposed regulation might undermine the twenty-four-hour rule of the air carriers; still others said it was almost impossible to define the nature and the quantity of the alcoholic beverages to which the proposed rule would refer.

On January 20, 1967, the agency announced that, after consideration of the comments received, it had concluded that the best course would be to disseminate, as widely as possible, information on the adverse effects of alcoholic beverages on crew member performance. With this announcement, the agency withdrew its proposal to tighten up the rules governing drinking. In their place, an advisory circular was being prepared to "apprise airmen of the problem and set forth the course of action that the agency is able to recommend on the basis of present knowledge."

Late in December, 1966, Dr. Stanley R. Mohler, Chief of FAA's Aeromedical Applications Division, Office of Aviation Medicine, had called a private meeting at FAA headquarters of representatives of the various pilot organizations and general aviation on the subject of drinking. Dr. Mohler distributed copies of his paper, "Recent Findings on the Impairment of Airmanship by Alcohol," in which he reported that ethyl alcohol was associated with one-third of all fatal general aviation accidents in 1963. Dr. Mohler said that an aggressive airmen education program was the best way to accomplish a reduction in this accident rate. He discussed both statistics and specific incidents, reporting, for example, that in one midwestern area during 1963, half of the ten fatal light-plane accidents involved alcohol. One was caused by a businessman who had drunk so much alcohol that his speech was markedly slurred in his communications with flight service station personnel. He made repeated passes at a hard-surfaced runway, which was at least 4,000 feet long, but was unable to land. A short time later, the businessman-pilot made his fatal landing when the airplane ran out of fuel.

Dr. Mohler reached three conclusions: (1) One ounce of whiskey or one beer consumed immediately preceding a flight can cause a significant impairment in airmanship; (2) evidence indicates that about one-third of the fatal accidents in civil light aircraft are caused directly or indirectly by ethyl alcohol ingestion; and (3) an aggressive education program for general aviation airmen is indicated.

Alcohol is not the only chemical that can effect an airman's ability to perform his duties. On July, 1963, the FAA issued a basic medical guide to the effects of various drugs on piloting duties—*Guide to Drug Hazards and Aviation Medicine*—prepared for FAA by Dr. Windsor C. Cutting, Professor of Therapeutics at Stanford University. The *Guide* listed all commonly used drugs, both those sold over-the-counter and those sold only by prescription.

EDUCATION AND ENFORCEMENT

The FAA has not been remiss in its safety educational work among general aviation pilots. In July, 1965, the agency awarded a $268,635 contract to the Flight Safety Foundation "to develop and apply an education program which will persuade the general aviation segment of the aviation community to upgrade its flight proficiency and knowledge in order to reduce the number of aircraft accidents." The program, called General Aviation Pilot Education, or GAPE for short, was designed to solve the main problem behind most general aviation accidents in recent years—lack of pilot proficiency and knowledge of safe flight procedures and practices, responsible for almost 80 per cent of the more than 5,000 general aviation accidents recorded in 1964. Major General Joseph D. Caldara, USAF (ret.) had been in charge of flight safety for the Air Force, where he had a spectacular record of success in reducing the accident rate. After retiring from the Air Force, General Caldara was put in charge of Project GAPE. As part of his campaign to make pilots aware of their inadequacies, he issued several strong statements on the subject of pilots' lack of skills, which drew criticism from some professional pilot groups. The FAA was criticized by the Aircraft Owners and Pilots Association

(AOPA) for "adverse publicity generated by the FAA contract with the Flight Safety Foundation." The FAA had claimed that there were 5,000 aviation accidents in 1964. This was translated by some newspaper correspondents into meaning that there were five thousand private plane crashes. One wire service confused the Project GAPE press release with earlier FAA statements on drinking and private flying accidents. "The press release," said AOPA, "did not explain that many of the accidents included in this figure were of a minor nature—hundreds were little more than 'fender bumpings.' "

Victor J. Kayne, head of AOPA's Office of Policy Coordination, wrote FAA Administrator McKee: "We hope that the FAA will take action to stop or counteract this adverse publicity." A press aide replied for General McKee: "We do not feel that it would be in the public interest to attempt to take action to stop or counteract the adverse publicity which resulted from the GAPE contract." This reply did not satisfy Mr. Kayne, and he sent a second letter to Administrator McKee, complaining that AOPA's primary concern was not with the general aviation accident statistics themselves, but with the distorted picture presented to the public. FAA's own figures refuted the claim that the general aviation fatality rate was any worse than that for commercial air carriers. Distorted information was seriously hurting the general aviation industry.

Mr. Kayne's second letter was answered directly by Administrator McKee: "I appreciate your candid letter of August 16, expressing concern that there is distortion in the general aviation picture as presented to the public in the Flight Safety Foundation's general aviation pilot education program. . . . To avoid misinterpretation, I have instructed responsible staff officers to take particular care to avoid ambiguity in statements used in press releases relating to the GAPE program. I am also sure that the Flight Safety Foundation does not want any misinterpretation of this program and I will discuss this matter with General Caldara."

Many suggestions are received by FAA from the public on how air safety could be better improved. One frequent contributor of suggestions has been the Airways Club, a New York-based organization made up of outspoken air travelers. Late in 1964, the club suggested that all airline passengers be assessed 20 cents per airline ticket to pay for installing arresting-gear equipment. According to *Aviation Daily,* an FAA technician, who had been working on an arresting-gear project for several months, commented dryly on this suggestion: "Well, it's novel." The Airport Operators Council was also skeptical about this ticket tax, as well as about the value of arresting gear. "The only ones who would benefit from the Airways Club idea, on the basis of what we know now, would be the landing gear manufacturers," the council told the *Daily.*

Enforcement of regulations, whether it be the drinking rules or one of the more controversial Federal Air Regulations, which often seem to pilots to impinge on their command authority, has always been a difficult job for the FAA. In many cases, the enforcement complaint against an airman rests on an interpretation of a rule that can be read more than one way, and the airman takes advantage of his right to appeal. In such cases, it is not uncommon for the FAA to be overruled. The Des Plaines, Illinois, pilot who paid a $150 fine in 1964 for making an unauthorized parachute jump while intoxicated was probably glad to get off so lightly on appeal.

On a different level, so to speak, was an enforcement appeal involving the suspension for forty-five days of the air transport rating of a transcontinental jet pilot who continued on across the country to his destination after having had to shut down one engine because of a fire warning. On January 6, 1967, the Civil Aeronautics Board upheld an earlier decision of its examiner that reversed the FAA's suspension order.

The violation charged by the FAA occurred on March 14, 1964, in the course of a scheduled nonstop commercial flight to Los Angeles. In addition to the normal DC-8 crew complement, a United Air Lines company pilot was conducting an official flight check. Approximately one hour after departure, with the jet about fifteen minutes away from O'Hare Airport in Chicago, there was a fire warning on number three engine, and the command pilot initiated emergency procedures. These included shutting down the engine. Both during and after the fire warning, there was no other indication that a fire had in fact occurred, and two inspections of the engine from inside the plane failed to show any evidence of fire. This was not too surprising to the command pilot and his crew. They were aware that a considerable number of false fire alarms had been experienced with the DC-8 jets.

After shutting down the engine, the pilot conferred both with his crew and the company observer as to what was to be done. He also consulted the company manual containing the applicable regulation. United's dispatcher at Chicago was contacted by radio, and, after the situation had been evaluated, it was agreed that the flight should continue. One reason supporting this decision was that good weather prevailed all across the United States. Accordingly, the plane by-passed five airports suitable for emergency jet landings and arrived four and-one-half hours later at Los Angeles.

According to the appropriate Federal Air Regulation, the pilot in command of a multi-engine aircraft is permitted to continue to an airport of his selection after failure of one engine "if he determines such action to be as safe a course of action as landing at the nearest suitable airport in point of time." It was the FAA administrator's contention in filing the violation notice that the chief pilot had "abused his discretion." This was disputed by the pilot, and the CAB hearing examiner found that "the record clearly establishes that the respondent considered all the factors and properly determined that none of them would affect the safety of the continued flight."

The board went on to say that not only was the text of the regulation "ambiguous," but that previous interpretations placed on the regulation "militate against the construction here urged by the Administrator."

The CAB noted that, before this particular regulation had been issued, when one engine became inoperative in a four-engine aircraft, it was mandatory for the pilot to land the aircraft at the nearest suitable airport. This requirement resulted in a pilot practice of failing to shut down malfunctioning engines in order to permit continuation of a flight—an unsafe practice, which lead to the amendment of the regulations "to permit the continuation of a flight with one engine inoperative under specific conditions."

Although determination of cause is CAB's—and now the National Transportation Safety Board's—responsibility, FAA plays an important role in the investigation of aircraft accidents, a role dating back to May, 1928, when the Department of Commerce established a board to determine the cause of aircraft accidents and placed the board under the direction of its Aeronautics Branch. In September, 1928, the civil aviation accident statistics published by the Aeronautics Branch, covering the first half of 1928, reported a total of 390 aircraft accidents, of which 34 occurred in scheduled flying, 69 in student instructions, 17 in experimental operations, and 270 in "miscellaneous" flying. Probable cause was pilot error in nearly half of the accidents, with power plant failure accounting for 16.59 percent, weather for 10.23 per cent, and airport or terrain for 8.72 per cent. The 390 accidents caused a total of 153 deaths and 276 injuries. Only six of the fatalities occurred as the result of scheduled transport flying.

The FAA in its 1963 annual report to Congress included a

detailed study of aviation accidents during calendar year 1962, the eleventh consecutive year in which the airline fatality rate stayed below 1 per 100 million passenger miles traveled.

FAA also reported that general aviation (non-airline civil aviation and private flying) accident rates had remained relatively stable over the past decade but had shown some improvement in recent years. Rates computed on the basis of 100,000 hours flown indicated that there were 36 accidents and 3.2 fatal accidents for calendar year 1962 compared with 36.5 and 3.3 for the preceding year. Based on plane miles flown, the figures for 1962 indicated that there were 2.8 accidents per million miles flown, as compared to 2.6 accidents per million miles in 1961. The general aviation fatality rate per million flight miles was the same for 1962 and 1961: 0.25. The 1963 report stated that, "encouraging as it appears when compared with the past, or with other modes of travel, the national air safety record leaves no room for complacence."

In its annual report to Congress for fiscal 1965, FAA reported no important change in the safety record of either the air carrier industry or general aviation. Although the accident fatality rates fluctuate from year to year, these fluctuations occur within a very narrow range. "The existence of the fluctuation shows that chance and human fallibility have not been entirely eliminated from aviation," the report went on to say. "The narrowness of the fluctuation range, together with the low figures for the rates involved, show that safety measures have achieved a high degree of effectiveness."

VII

Certification of Airmen and Aircraft

Some 480,000 Americans currently hold pilot certificates. These range from student pilot certificates, through private and commercial pilot certificates to air transport certificates. Student pilots are given a certificate which strictly limits the kind of flying they may do. A student pilot may not carry passengers, nor may a student pilot undertake a cross-country flight without close supervision of an FAA-licensed instructor. Private pilots, on the other hand, may both carry passengers and make unrestricted cross-country flights, but they may not do any flying for hire. Commercial and air transport pilots are considered professionals, and are entitled to charge for their services. At the same time, they are required to meet higher standards of skill and proficiency, as well as to pass more frequent and more demanding federally supervised medical examinations.

Under FAA rules, different ratings are required for pilots flying different types of aircraft—single engine and multi-engine land or seaplanes, helicopters, gliders, and balloons. Nearly one thousand pilots hold ratings which permit them to fly helicopters and other rotorcraft only. After extensive training and careful testing, private, commercial, and air transport pilots can obtain ratings which permit them to fly by reference to the instruments in their cockpit only.

Not all airmen are pilots, however. Mechanics, parachute riggers, ground instructors, dispatchers, airport traffic controllers, flight radio operators, navigators, and engineers are included in FAA's airmen category. Each of these must pass a detailed federal examination to obtain his FAA certificate. Flight schools, ground schools, and mechanic's schools are also certificated by the FAA, as are the instructors who teach in them.

The FAA Aeronautical Center in Oklahoma City serves as the central storage depot for all airmen and aircraft records. More than a million airmen licenses and ratings are maintained in the electronic filing system and more than 130,000 aircraft records, including all active civil aircraft in the United States. It is possible for a prospective purchaser of an airplane, for example, to have a quick search made at the FAA record center to determine whether there are any outstanding mortgages against the plane or whether the seller is giving clear title to the aircraft. Examinations taken by airmen throughout the nation are sent to the Oklahoma City central records office for grading before the student is licensed. All the tests given pilots, radio operators, ground instructors, navigators, flight engineers, and aviation mechanics are prepared at the Aeronautical Center. This is a never-ending task, since no examination is permitted to remain unchanged for more than three months.

CERTIFICATION OF PILOTS

To obtain a pilot's license, a student pilot must obtain a medical certificate from a doctor approved by FAA and then pass a series of tests, including a lengthy written examination and an extensive flight test. Before the flight test can be taken, the student pilot must have had a required number of hours of both dual instruction and solo flight. When all the tests and examinations are completed to the satisfaction of the FAA, the student is rewarded with a private pilot's license. To qualify for a commercial license, and finally an air transport rating, the private pilot must invest many more hours in study and in actual flight.

Despite the difficulties and the expense of qualifying for even the private pilot license, FAA reports a continuing boom in private flying. During 1966, for example, there was a spectacular 34 per cent increase in the number of new pilot certificates—188,530, as compared to 141,007 certificates issued in 1965. The interest in private flying in the United States has snowballed steadily since 1960. In 1965, California had the greatest number of licensed pilots—69,501, followed by Texas with 34,822, New York with 25,361, and Illinois with 24,659.

During 1966, the FAA certificated 129,180 student pilots, 42,464 private pilots, 14,210 commercial pilots, and 3,378 airline transport pilots. In the ten years between 1956 and 1965, the agency issued 1.3 million airmen certificates of all kinds, both for flyers and for nonflyers. The issuing and handling of this volume of records, an enormous task in itself, is complicated by the fact that certificates are issued for an indefinite duration, making it impracticable to keep records current and to maintain a separate file of active airmen. To correct this situation, the FAA began automating its system of issuing airman certificates in 1963 and using electronic data processing equipment to maintain its files. The FAA also dropped the rule requiring airmen to submit up-to-date experience data every two years. The most immediate benefit to the airman was consolidation of all his privileges, ratings, and medical qualifications on one certificate in lieu of the various separate certificates under the former system.

During fiscal 1965, the FAA tightened up its pilot training and certification regulations for pilots flying general aviation jets. A general aviation jet standards board was established, composed of FAA technical personnel with a knowledge of problems associated with jet aircraft in service or about to join the active general aviation fleet. This board was made responsible for developing and recommending guide-lines, policies, standards, and procedures for type ratings, for six-month checks, for transition and recurrent training, and for recommending solutions for business jet operational problems. At the same time, the FAA took a major step for-ward in its program to upgrade private pilot performance and improve the general aviation safety record by focusing on the qualifications and supervision of flight instructors. In 1964, a new flight instructor handbook was issued emphasiz-ing what the FAA called "recognized principles of effective teaching and efficient flight instruction procedures." This handbook was made the basis for a new practical test for all applicants for original certification as a flight instructor. In addition, requalification of all flight instructors is now re-quired every two years. To requalify, a flight instructor is required to demonstrate currency and competence as well as satisfactory performance as an active flight instructor. The amendment also requires flight instructors to assume addi-tional responsibilities for the supervision of student pilot solo flight operations.

Two major research projects on primary flight training were established during fiscal 1965. One involved the possi-ble use of ground trainers for certain elementary flight train-ing maneuvers, the other was aimed at determining the value of primary flight training in airplanes equipped with full-time stability control augmentation systems. The agency also began exploring, together with industry, ways of increasing the percentage of student pilots that successfully complete their training and receive private pilot certificates. In 1965, only one student pilot in three was going on to obtain his private license.

On June 28, 1965, the FAA resolved a long standing ques-tion as to the status of flight examiners who ride aboard air-craft for the purpose of testing pilots. Since the regulations clearly provide that a student may not under any circumstances carry passengers while he is in command of an aircraft, it was not clear whether the student pilot or the inspector was in command. To avoid placing inspectors in a position of responsibility without necessarily having full authority, the FAA ruled that "an inspector or other authorized flight examiner conducting a flight test is an observer, and normally not pilot-in-command."

Instrument flying involves two basic types of proficiency. One is the ability to handle the aircraft without visual reference to the ground or other outside points, that is, to be able to fly the plane entirely by reference to the instruments within the cockpit. The second type of proficiency requires that the pilot manage his airplane under these conditions in accordance with the instrument flight rules laid down by the FAA and that the pilot maintain communication with the FAA at all times, filing position reports and periodic changes in flight plan. It is this last portion of FAA's instrument flight rules that many private pilots find burdensome. An FAA experimental program, known as IFR-SIP (Instrument Flight Rules–Systems Indoctrination Program) was designed to overcome a pilot's feeling that he has somehow become enmeshed in red tape while making instrument flights. Under the IFR-SIP program, air traffic control radar service is provided to each pilot to the maximum extent possible. The pilot is briefed frequently on his exact position, as determined by radar, and advised of the distance to his designation. In addition, special preflight and inflight services are provided pilots operating under the program. All pilots must do to get this special service is request SIP assistance when filing an IFR flight plan. Many instrument-rated pilots are reluctant to fly on instruments because they believe the system is too complicated for their limited experience. However, the FAA believes that pilots who participate in the program will find the system far less complicated than they imagined and will become so proficient they will be able to fly on instruments in the future with increasing confidence.

Because of the widely differing characteristics of piston aircraft and turbine-powered planes, the FAA announced in 1965 that it would issue rules requiring flight engineers to obtain ratings for the particular class of aircraft on which they served. The new rules required flight engineers to have a rating for at least one of three classes of airplanes: piston engine, turboprop, or turbojet.

The FAA also re-evaluated its enforcement policy as it affects airmen so that, for minor infractions of the rules, field inspectors could issue warning notices on the spot. The new warning notices save time, provide a simple means of letting the violator know the disposition of his case, and serve as a record as well as a source of statistical enforcement data.

The agency has also become concerned over the increasing number and the seriousness of overseas violations involving U.S.-certificated airmen and U.S.-registered aircraft. To combat the problem, the FAA in 1965 undertook investigations covering the two geographical areas where the majority of the incidents were occurring—the Caribbean area and Europe.

Violations reported in the domestic enforcement program during fiscal 1965 totaled 4,980. Of the actions processed to completion during the year, 1,309 involved suspension or revocation of certificates. Approximately 8 per cent of the airmen involved appealed the FAA decision to the Civil Aeronautics Board (CAB).

THE RIGHT OF APPEAL

An airman who violates the federal air regulations through reckless flying or through other rule-breaking activities may have his pilot's license suspended or revoked. In such cases, a series of appeal procedures are available, to make certain that the airman's rights are protected.

If the airman requests a formal hearing, the FAA attorney presents a case against him, and the airman is given opportunity to present evidence in his own defense, either orally or in the form of documents. Each side has the right of cross-examination. At the conclusion of the hearing, the FAA hearing officer makes his decision on the basis of the evidence presented. He may dismiss the complaint against the airman, or he may issue an order amending, modifying, suspending, or revoking the airman's certificate. If the airman is not satisfied with the hearing officer's decision, he may appeal the case to the National Transportation Safety Board in the Department of Transportation. The Safety Board calls for a new hearing before one of its own examiners. In this hearing, the FAA must prove its case against the airman all over again. If the Safety Board finds that the airman is not guilty as charged, the board has the authority to set aside the FAA suspension or revocation. Should the airman be dissatisfied with the Safety Board's decision he still has the right to take the case to a federal appeals court for further review. Before the Safety Board was established in 1967, pilots had the right to appeal to the Civil Aeronautics Board. CAB's way was to establish the facts in the case in what amounted to a new proceeding against the airman, and the FAA would, in effect, act as a prosecutor in defending its original decision. The very act of appeal often was advantageous to the airman, since the FAA almost invariably preferred to compromise a penalty rather than to prepare evidence, take testimony, and defend itself before the CAB. Most of the appeals involved such matters as a pilot landing on instruments when instrument landing visibility was below the minimum, or a pilot flying through clouds in a control zone, or a private pilot charging for flight services.

One interesting case involved the appeal of an instrument-rated private pilot against a thirty-day suspension order. The pilot had been suspended while a student. On a night flight between Lexington, Kentucky, and Indianapolis, Indiana, he had been caught in weather conditions which were less than the minimums prescribed for the flight. The facts, according to the record, were that the student had checked his weather, which indicated that he should have no trouble on the flight although he might encounter scattered clouds. After proceeding on his course over these scattered clouds, he suddenly noticed that he was above an almost solid cloud cover, and the ground was obscured. At about this same time, he realized that he was making very slow progress. Upon checking with an FAA flight service station by radio, he was advised he was flying into headwinds of more than fifty miles an hour. The student pilot then radioed to Weir Cook Field near Indianapolis, and was advised that a field northeast of his position was open. A calculation showed that he did not have enough fuel to reach that field. The ground station then told him that in order to obtain help in descending through the cloud layer, he would have to declare an emergency. The student pilot did this and was guided through the cloud layer by precision radar, landing safely at Weir Cook Field. Because he had allowed himself to be trapped on top of the clouds and had had to make, in effect, an instrument descent, he was charged with violating the Federal Air Regulations. On appeal, the Civil Aeronautics Board reversed the administrator's thirty-day suspension, stating that the facts "indicate the respondent became involved, through no apparent fault of his own, in a situation where it was not an unreasonable course of action to declare an emergency and descend through the broken cloud layer. His actions endangered no other aircraft and, indeed, there appears to be a serious question as to whether a violation of the Federal Air Regulations in fact occurred."

Another recent case involved an emergency order revoking an airman's commercial pilot certificate on the grounds that he had obtained the certificate through false entries in his log book. Federal Air Regulations require that a total of 200 hours of flight time is necessary to obtain a commercial pilot's certificate, unless the applicant is a graduate of a certificated flight school, in which case, the requirement is reduced to 160 hours. The airman appealed his certificate revocation. The hearing examiner found that the airman had overstated his time in the case of fifty-two solo flights, and that nine of the flights entered in the log were never flown. (The examiner also found that the airman had made opposite errors in other entries, which had the effect of understating his flight time by one hour and five minutes!)

The FAA would not have had occasion to question the log book entries if the airman had not had a falling-out with the school that was training him to become a commercial pilot. The airman's contract called for payment of $2,445 to cover the total cost of instruction and flight time, to be paid in installments of $300 a month. When the airman stopped tuition payments, the school asked the FAA to investigate the student's flight time. This disclosed a discrepancy between the school records and the log book figures. The explanation offered by the airman was that in order to keep costs down he had falsified the school records. However, the CAB examiner found to the contrary, and the board upheld the FAA's revocation action.

AEROMEDICAL ASPECTS OF CERTIFICATION

Medical examinations are required of all pilots except glider pilots, who must certify, however, that they have no incapacitating physical defects. Private pilots are required to have a complete physical examination at least once every two years; commercial pilots must be examined at least once every year; and air transport pilots must be examined every six months. Although not required by the FAA, most commercial airlines also require that their pilots be periodically examined by the company's physician.

If a medical examination discloses a condition which could result in the sudden incapacitation of a pilot, his certificate to fly is revoked. Such grounding can result from disclosure of heart disease, chronic alcoholism, drug addiction, or mental disorder. The FAA at times permits airmen who have a disqualifying medical disability to demonstrate that they are able to compensate for these conditions. In these cases, they may receive a third-class medical certificate, making them eligible for a private license, either on the basis of demonstrated ability or by waiving the regulations. The FAA never grants such exemptions to airline pilots.

Pilots of all classes must now take their medical examinations from physicians specifically designated by the FAA as aviation medical examiners. In a 1960 aeromedical decision, the regulations were changed so that all applicants for a student or a private pilot license could take medical examinations only from FAA-designated aviation medical examiners instead of from any registered physician. To provide adequate regional coverage, FAA made over 2,000 appointments of authorized examiners, bringing the total number at the end of 1960 to 4,268. To bring the examiner into closer relationship with the agency, and to give him a fuller understanding of FAA purposes, programs, and problems, the agency began publication of a monthly *Medical Newsletter*. An aviation medical examiner training program was also developed.

The number of physicians designated as aviation medical examiners totaled 5,682 at the end of fiscal 1965. In addition, senior flight surgeons at 546 military bases were designated by FAA to perform medical examinations for military personnel applying for civil medical certificates. Ten three-day seminars were held for the instruction of aviation medical examiners, at which 1,625 doctors were trained in modern aeromedical concepts, certification procedures and practices, and accident investigation techniques. During fiscal 1965, designated aviation medical examiners performed 311,707 physical examinations. In 12,428 of these examinations, there were reports of new pathology of significance in the certification process; 8,712 applications were denied. Requests for reconsideration of the denials totaled 921. In 741 cases, the Federal Air Surgeon upheld denial; in 180 cases, the decision was reversed. As a final resort, a denied applicant may petition the administrator for exemption from the established medical standards. The administrator is assisted in reviewing such petitions by a medical advisory panel composed of specialists from private practice. During fiscal 1965, the administrator waived the standards for 82 petitioners and denied certification to 257.

FAA requires that airline transport pilots engaged in passenger carrying operations submit an annual electrocardiographic tracing for medical review. Some 16,640 such tracings were received during fiscal year 1965; of this number, 31 showed evidence of myocardial infarction, which is a cause for denial of medical certification, pending additional evaluation.

CERTIFICATION OF AIRCRAFT

By the end of 1966, there were 106,337 registered civil aircraft operating in the United States. These ranged from small single-seat sport planes—in some cases home-built—to giant multi-engine jet transports and included helicopters, balloons, blimps, gliders—anything, according to the FAA, that flies "this side of outer space and is capable of carrying a man." U.S. commercial airlines were operating 2,337 planes. All other civil aircraft were in a category known as "general aviation": corporate aircraft used for business trips, personal aircraft that may be used part-time for business and part-time for pleasure trips, air taxi aircraft that carry passengers and cargo for hire, airplanes used to spray crops for weed and insect control, aircraft for pipeline and forest patrol, highway survey and aerial photography aircraft, police and other law enforcement aircraft, and aircraft operated for instructional purposes. Each of these planes carried an FAA certificate of airworthiness.

The task of obtaining this certificate begins the moment the plane's manufacturer starts work on the design at his drawing board. FAA aeronautical engineers work side by side with factory engineers on the drawings and calculations of each new aircraft. Throughout the entire building process, they check the progress of the components—fuselage, wings, landing gear, tail surfaces, and so on—both for quality of workmanship and for conformity with the approved design. The same watchfulness is exercised by the FAA over the design and manufacture of aircraft engines, propellers, instruments, even the interior configuration of the aircraft— seat locations, mountings, seat belts, the size and location of windows, doors, and emergency exits.

When the first aircraft built from the new design, called the "prototype," is finished, it is not allowed to fly immediately. The FAA requires that it first undergo a series of ground tests. The aircraft is taxied out onto a ramp and the engines are run up, although they already have been tested many hundreds of hours. At varying speeds, the plane is taxied around the field and up and down the runways, while the test pilot proves out the flight controls—ailerons, rudders, and elevators. In some tests, the prototype aircraft are actually destroyed in the process of gathering essential data on structural strength and safety. Only after all these ground performance tests show that the aircraft measures up to standards set by the FAA, is the approval to fly given and the plane granted an "experimental certificate of airworthiness."

Prototype aircraft are subjected to the roughest treatment, to make certain that they can stand overloads and sudden stresses. Sometimes as many as four aircraft will be used in the prototype testing, confirming design calculations and evaluating performance, flight characteristics, and mechanical, hydraulic, and electrical systems under actual operating conditions. Usually the interior of the prototype aircraft is unfinished. In place of seats, special calibration equipment is installed and tanks of water or sandbags are carried as ballast. By adding or removing ballast, the weight-carrying characteristics of the aircraft in flight are determined.

In the case of a new transport aircraft, the flight test program can last six months or longer. At the end of the successful program, the FAA issues a "type certificate" and a "production certificate." Each aircraft that conforms to the type certificate is granted an airworthiness certificate. The FAA's type certificate acknowledges the fact that the airplane has met the prescribed standards of construction and performance; the production certificate attests to the manufacturer's ability to duplicate the approved design; the airworthiness certificate is the FAA's way of acknowledging that the airplane conforms to the type certificate and is safe for commercial service. Every airplane that follows the original off the assembly line earns its own individual certificate of airworthiness through an actual series of flight tests. Small aircraft get the same attention during design, construction, testing, and production as do large planes.

FAA's interest in the aircraft does not end with the issuance of a certificate of airworthiness. Once an aircraft begins flying, the FAA continues to be concerned with its operational safety, with such matters as the qualifications of the men who do the maintenance work on the plane and where and how it is done. FAA monitors airline maintenance programs, approving the times for periodic inspection and overhaul of various aircraft components. If an unsafe condition develops after the aircraft enters commercial service, the FAA notifies all operators of the same type of plane of the problem and the recommended or required corrective action. The agency may also require that corrective action be taken within a specified period of time. In rare emergency cases, the FAA may order the aircraft grounded until corrective action is taken.

Regulations require that all inspections, repairs, and alterations, whether major or minor, made on any aircraft or its components, be entered in a permanent record. To facilitate this, every aircraft and every engine is identified by a serial number, and each has its own log book—an individual record of its performance that remains with it throughout its service life. Whenever an airplane flies, an entry is made in its log. If a carburetor is changed, it is noted in the engine log. If a propeller has to be removed for balancing, that too is noted.

Sometimes, despite these elaborate precautions, an airplane develops a defect which is revealed only when an accident or a series of incidents occur. Such accidents occurred in 1960, when Lockheed's new turboprop transport, the Electra, twice suffered wing failure in midair. It is very rare for any aircraft to suffer inflight wing failure, because defects almost always show up in the course of the elaborate test work that is done on the wing structure before even the first prototype is allowed to fly.

Potential defects in aircraft with considerable service are detected through regular maintenance care. Most wing failure accidents occur when an aircraft encounters very severe turbulence with forces so great that they literally tear the plane apart, but the Electra accidents did not seem to fall into this category. Previous FAA records revealed only five cases of commercial airliners losing their wings in the air, and four of these involved not structural weakness but extreme turbulence, which caused the aircraft to maneuver so violently that the wing design limits were exceeded. After the second accident involving wing failure on an Electra, the FAA was under considerable pressure to ground the entire fleet of Electras, but decided instead to limit their speed to 275 knots. It has long been known that aircraft speeds add to the structural load of an aircraft during turbulence. The 275 knot limitation was arbitrary and not based on any particular scientific data. However, the restriction was effective, and no additional Electras suffered wing failure.

An intensive investigation by both Lockheed and FAA scientists finally disclosed that the Electra developed a severe vibration problem at certain engine speeds. The solution was to return each of the Electras to the Lockheed factory, where a substantially new and stronger wing structure was retro-fitted. This retrofit program was costly, not only to Lockheed but to the airlines that suffered schedule interruptions, but no other accidents occurred, and later the Electra became known as one of the safest airplanes in the sky.

The FAA has a novel program of flexible reliability control methods for airframes, power plants, and other components for transport aircraft. This concept assures a continuous high level of airworthiness, and at the same time allows the air carriers to remain in control of the maintenance activities. As an example, the FAA cites one turbine engine that is allowed to operate 6,400 hours between overhauls. The reduced number of shutdowns per 1,000 engine operating hours provides factual evidence of improved reliability. The new standards are sufficiently broad to permit individual airlines to adapt them to existing maintenance programs. There was good participation among the trunk carriers in applying the reliability control concept in 1965. At year's end, steps were being taken to extend the concept to the small trunk carriers and local service airlines, and serious consideration was being given to extending it to certain general aviation aircraft.

FAA has access to the performance records of the airlines and requires air carriers to file mechanical reliability reports (MRR's), listing specific aircraft component failures, as well as malfunctions and defects that might endanger safety operations. All such reports are processed by computer and made available within ten days of the close of each operating month. All data are reviewed by FAA engineers and operations and maintenance personnel. FAA statisticians develop trend rates and other useful information from this data. As an example of the usefulness of such information, the FAA reported in 1963 that one of the first conclusions that emerged from a review of the MRR's was that fire-warning systems on air carrier aircraft were malfunctioning at a completely unacceptable rate. Malfunctioning usually took the form of a false fire warning. The FAA investigated and discovered three principal causes: (1) inadequate maintenance techniques, (2) weakness of engineering design, and (3) lack of coordination between the manufacturers of fire detection equipment and the air carrier operators. Results of the study were made available to appropriate personnel, together with corrective recommendations. During fiscal 1965, 8,364 MRR's were submitted by industry and processed by the agency; eighty-five corrective actions were initiated for industry-wide action.

As of July 1, 1961, there were 824 aircraft repair stations certificated by the FAA. By the end of fiscal 1963 the number had grown to 1,070, and was increasing at the rate of 120 per year. The annual volume of maintenance and overhaul work performed by these stations has been estimated at $500 million.

HOMEMADE AIRPLANES AND OTHER MATTERS

While certification of commercial aircraft designs gets most of the FAA's attention, and properly so, the FAA also has a responsibility for issuing airworthiness certificates to home-built planes. This responsibility goes back to 1947 when a Portland, Oregon, amateur plane builder, George Bogardus, flew his home-built airplane, the "Little GB" to Washington, D.C., to persuade the Civil Aeronautics Board to amend the rules so that amateurs could build aircraft for education and recreation. The CAB listened to Mr. Bogardus. It was impressed by the quality of work in his home-built plane, so the rules were amended to permit a home builder to do just about anything he wanted, from constructing airframes to rebuilding or even manufacturing power plants. No license was needed. All a home builder had to do was get his plane approved for flight when it was completed. A separate branch in FAA now handles certification of home-built aircraft; its basic duty is to protect the public from non-airworthy planes.

In a practical way, the members of this branch also served as friendly advisers to all who are known to be building homemade aircraft. The rules do not require the home craftsman to advise the FAA that he plans to build a plane or that he has a plane under construction. Even so, most of them keep the local FAA inspector advised and often confer with him about details. Before the final covering is put on the plane, the FAA inspector is usually invited to take a look at the interior. This generally makes a later tear-down inspection unnecessary. Inspectors keep a watch on construction details and are often present during the first flight of the aircraft. The FAA usually writes a specially tailored set of operating limitations for each home-built plane. For the first few flying hours, an experimental home-built plane must be operated away from populated areas, but eventually the homemade aircraft is awarded an operating placard and a set of operating limitations. If there is room, it may even be allowed to carry passengers.

With the advent of the jet age, FAA's job of certifying new

aircraft increased markedly. During 1960, the agency issued thirty-six type certificates for new aircraft and approved sixty-seven new engines and forty-three propellers, including twelve certificates for transport aircraft, eighteen for private or business aircraft, five for helicopters, and one for a glider. Four years later, in fiscal 1964, type certificates were issued for forty-four new aircraft models, forty-nine propellers, and ninety-eight aircraft engines, including one rocket engine and fourteen turbine types. Approximately 10,000 original and export airworthiness certificates were processed, and 1,168 supplemental type certificates, required for changes in aircraft type designs. FAA inspectors conducted surveillance of factory operations and quality control systems for some 833 manufacturers.

The Boeing 727 tri-jet, which later was to have problems with its high sink rate, was certificated during this period, as were the Beech King Air, the first U.S. light twin-turboprop business aircraft to be certificated, and the Sikorsky S-61N twin-turbine helicopter.

Also during fiscal 1964, FAA amended its procedures for certification of surplus military aircraft to foster the economic development of remote areas in Alaska. An unprecedented exemption was granted to Alaskan operators to permit them to use C-82 flying boxcars for commercial flight operations. The C-82 is a World War II cargo airplane, certificated by FAA in the restricted category.

As an indication of what a certificated aircraft, properly maintained, can produce in the way of revenue mileage, North Central Airlines retired DC-3 number N 21728, in March, 1966, after it had flown more than 12 million miles. The ground taxi time on the aircraft alone totaled well over 100,000 miles. It had burned nearly 8 million gallons of gasoline and worn out 25,000 spark plugs, 550 tires, and 136 engines. This North Central DC-3 was built at the Douglas facility at Santa Monica, California, on August 11, 1939, and

was one of the earliest of 11,000 such twin-engine air transports built by Douglas. Retirement from scheduled service,
however, does not mean the end of N 21728. North Central
continues to use her as a flying test bed and sometimes as an
executive aircraft for company officials.

VIII

Research and Development

The Federal Aviation Administration is not a basic research agency. The National Aeronautics and Space Administration (NASA) has this responsibility for aeronautics—although some in aviation say that NASA has neglected aircraft research to concentrate almost entirely on the more challenging problems of space flight. Most of FAA's research is of the applied variety, such as its research into methods of arresting an aircraft by external means to prevent over-run accidents. Some FAA research consists of little more than statistical exercises, like the study made in preparation for a proposed reduction in aircraft separation on transatlantic crossings from 120 miles to 90 miles. The aeromedical research that led up to the FAA's rule against drinking before flying consisted for the most part of autopsies performed on pilots killed in crashes.

In the public hearings held during the first half of 1966 on the North Atlantic separation question, airline pilots opposing the reduction in lateral separation distance did a surprisingly good job of demonstrating that at least that part of the FAA's statistical work could not stand the test of expert examination. On the other hand, the psychological studies on "circadian rhythm" by Dr. Sheldon Freud, an Air Force officer on loan to FAA, were well thought out and are today still unchallenged.

AEROMEDICAL RESEARCH

The studies on circadian rhythm—the phrase is taken from the Latin words *circa,* meaning around, and *dies,* meaning day—were undertaken to test the effect of abrupt time-zone changes on bodily functions, including certain functions relating to mental alertness and the ability to make judgments as well as to do routine work. This problem of time adjustment is believed to exist for all air travelers who move at jet speed across several time zones.

Some people's daily life cycle is upset merely by a change to daylight saving time. Others, like the crews of commercial jetliners, seem less affected by sudden time changes. It may be that jet crews learn to adjust to fast passage across a half-dozen time zones. The FAA doesn't know, but hopes to find out in follow-up experiments similar to the one conducted with a small group of volunteers who were flown east to Rome, west to Manila, and south to Santiago, Chile. The Santiago flight was for control purposes, since it entailed a presumably fatiguing jet flight of fourteen hours but no change of time zones. To establish their circadian norms, each subject was carefully observed for two weeks before his test flight. Similar examinations were made during the two weeks following the flight. Specially designed instruments were used for the continuous monitoring of body temperatures, heart functions, nervous tension, and other key bodily indicators. A battery of standard psychological tests was used to measure mental fatigue.

What did the tests show? FAA reports:

On the east and west flights, it was determined that three to five days were required for the human body to return to normal circadian periodicity, after arrival at the destination. Following the return flight, only about one day was required for return to normal. During the period of disrupted circadian rhythm, the ability of the subjects to perform specific tasks was lower than that of the subjects who made the long southward flight, which involved no change in time zones and no interrupted circadian function.

The aeromedical research program is primarily aimed at preventing aircraft accidents and at reducing the likelihood of injury or death when accidents do occur. Emphasis in the program is on human errors and limitations, in the belief that these are the primary causes of aircraft accidents. In 1960, the FAA established its Civil Aeromedical Research Institute at the University of Oklahoma at Norman, Oklahoma. The institute's clinical research branch located at Georgetown University Hospital, Washington, D.C., has accumulated data for two major projects: (1) a study of the effect of normal aging processes on civil air crew performance, and (2) a study of the hazards resulting from specific diseases in civil aircrew members.

Both studies involve data to be collected over a period of years. Subjects participating in the aging study are examined annually.

Among the special studies conducted at the Georgetown Clinical Research Institute during fiscal 1965 was one on the effect on airmen's vision of an eyedrop commonly used to treat glaucoma. The purpose of the study was to establish criteria to justify medical certification of certain airmen suffering from glaucoma. In another special study, thirty FAA test pilots were given medical and performance evaluations in which the examiners looked for evidence of excessive stress peculiar to test pilots. As long ago as 1963, the Civil Aeromedical Research Institute had developed a pocket-sized electroencephalograph for recording brain wave activity of pilots subject to unusual stress under actual flight conditions. FAA medical research teams in recent years have also investigated visual illusions that create hazardous conditions in flight and have probed the characteristics of vertigo, a critical but little understood factor in many general aviation accidents.

As an economy move, the FAA in April, 1966, announced that it would transfer its aeromedical research activities at the Georgetown Clinical Research Institute in Washington, D.C., to the Civil Aeromedical Research Institute in Oklahoma City.

FAA reported during fiscal 1965 that its researchers had obtained evidence that a significant number of crop-duster accidents had resulted from pilot exposure to the insecticides which they were applying. It appeared that a crop-duster's nervous system could suffer impairment as a result of exposure to many types of insecticide chemicals. Preventive measures were evolved, and information was made available to crop-duster groups.

A number of pilots who have suffered coronary occlusions are allowed to fly on the basis of FAA-granted exemptions from the medical standards. To provide a more definitive basis for granting these exemptions, FAA makes studies to determine the effect of specific exercise programs on the heart functions. The results are encouraging; objective tests indicate that exercise therapy for pilots who have experienced myocardial infarction is beneficial. Similar findings have been made in the case of pilots suffering from high blood pressure or hypertension.

The FAA has also studied the tolerances of the human head to impact forces, that is, to determine how much of a blow the head can tolerate in "survivable" accidents—defined as accidents in which the aircraft's frame remains intact. On the basis of this study, it was determined that the tolerance of the head is 200 G forces (or 200 times the force of gravity); the nose was determined to be able to withstand 30 G forces before fracture. These tolerances are an aid to aircraft design engineers, as witnessed by the fact that the instrument panel of one popular general aviation aircraft and the seat of one leading jet air transport plane have been redesigned as part of a program that the agency calls the delethalization of aircraft interiors.

In an effort to improve the survivability of pilots and crew members of light aircraft, FAA scientists have developed standards for appropriate attachment points for light aircraft shoulder harnesses, and have made these findings available to the aviation industry. It is interesting to note that the Civil Aeronautics Board estimated that during 1964 some 200 lives might have been saved if shoulder harnesses had been used in light aircraft.

Since 1964, the results of FAA's medical research program have been made available to scientists, scholars, and others in a series of aviation medical reports. Representative titles are "Pilot Fatigue," "Human Factors in Emergency Evacuation," and 'Studies of Aging in Aviation Personnel." Included in the series is a bibliography of 503 aviation medical papers and reports published by FAA and its predecessor agency, the CAA.

TURBULENCE

During fiscal 1965, the FAA and the National Aeronautics and Space Administration established a joint project called TAPER (Turbulent Air Pilot Environmental Research), whose purpose was to study both pilot and aircraft environment at the time of flight through turbulent air. Using specially-instrumented, swept-wing jets, both FAA and NASA pilots flew through areas of known turbulence to collect engineering data and to record their own impressions and responses. This information was then programmed into computers of special flight simulation capability. Using these computers, the pilots then 'flew" in simulated turbulence of much greater violence than they could safely fly through in reality. A report based on data from both real and simulated flights pointed out the need for improvements in instrumentation, control damping, longitudinal control, and trimming capabilities.

One of FAA's more interesting turbulence studies was conducted by the Flight Safety Foundation, which sought to determine whether a pattern existed in reported turbulence upsets that could provide clues to preventive measures. The most significant finding was that known upsets all occurred at night, or while the aircraft were being flown on instruments. Attention was accordingly focused on improving aircraft altitude instruments and cockpit display; seventeen airlines improved their attitude gyros and installed new and improved instruments and instrument panel lighting. In addition, FAA prepared a color film, entitled *Upset,* to supplement industry training efforts to solve the problems of flight into turbulence.

Although turbulence problems have plagued airmen since the days of the Wright brothers, it was not until rather recently that clear air turbulence became a problem. Mostly this phenomenon occurs at very high altitudes, but it is at these altitudes that today's swept-wing jets operate most efficiently. During 1963 and the first half of 1964, FAA reported one accident and several incidents involving upsets, or uncontrolled dives in jet aircraft that had experienced severe turbulence at high altitudes.

While emphasizing that flights should avoid turbulence areas if possible, FAA in an advisory circular urged pilots to concentrate on maintaining control over the attitude of their aircraft rather then attempting to correct erratic airspeed indications. To minimize the possibility of an aircraft stall and consequent loss of control, jet aircraft manufacturers revised upwards their recommended rough air penetration speeds. At the same time, as the FAA accelerated its research work into turbulence, air carriers began training their pilots to cope with the problems associated with jet turbulence penetration. One research project covered techniques for identifying, tracking, and displaying turbulence produced both in clear air and thunderstorms, and efforts were made to validate the effectiveness of improved airborne weather radar, electronic storm detectors, and a sensor designed to measure temperature changes in air masses. FAA also has been studying ways to make weather information visible to traffic controllers so that they can guide pilots around severe weather and keep from inadvertently directing traffic into bad weather areas. In a number of tests to determine pilot reaction to the high G forces encountered in areas of severe turbulence, airline pilots serve as subjects in a human centrifuge made available by the Navy's Aeromedical Acceleration Laboratory.

The FAA in 1965 awarded two research contracts, totaling $53,800, to accumulate better inflight data that would help pilots of swept-wing jets to deal more effectively with turbulence—one to obtain highly precise data on the response of pilots to aircraft turbulence encountered in regular jet airline service, the other to conduct a meteorological study of clear air turbulence.

One deadly form of clear air turbulence seems to prey on small planes exclusively. "Wing tip vortices" turbulence occurs when a large, powerful, multi-engine plane is flying at a high angle of attack but a slow speed, as during take-off or landing. Such an aircraft trails behind each wing tip a path of twin tornadoes, which can, and has, torn the wings off smaller planes that encounter them. To explain how to deal with this kind of turbulence and how to avoid it, even though it is not visible, the FAA in November, 1965, mailed a sixteen-page illustrated pamphlet to all licensed pilots who held current medical certificates. The pamphlet, intended primarily for pilots of light- to medium-size single and multi-engine aircraft, described in detail the hazards of wake turbulence—which pilots once erroneously called "prop wash."

PROJECT ACCORDION

FAA's research work often leads to changes in regulations. Because of the growing accuracy and dependability of electronic airborne and surface navigation aids used by the transatlantic air carriers, the FAA, as early as 1962, amended its rules for transatlantic flights by dropping the requirement that a certificated navigator be aboard during all air carrier flights. At about the same time, the FAA launched what it called Project Accordion, aimed at reducing the minimum separation distance of aircraft on the busier North Atlantic air routes. Project Accordion was a joint effort of the FAA, the U.S. Coast Guard, and the transatlantic airlines. The decision as to whether separation standards could be reduced depended on the navigational accuracy of the newly developed Doppler wind drift calculation system. Canadian and British shore-based radars were called upon to make position accuracy checks of aircraft navigating by the Doppler system. Additional data were obtained from two Coast Guard radar vessels, one moored between Labrador and Ireland, the other between Newfoundland and the Azores. FAA also used flight-inspection C-135 aircraft to evaluate the Doppler system as well as to flight-check the North Atlantic LORAN system.

Acting on FAA recommendations, and using Project Accordion data, the International Civil Aviation Organization (ICAO) in January, 1966, ordered a reduction in lateral separation between aircraft on the North Atlantic from 120 miles to 90 miles. Distrustful of the FAA's statistical "proof" that closer separation would be no threat to safety, some pilots flying the North Atlantic continued to insist on a lateral separation of 120 miles. In response to pilot criticism, FAA, in February, took the position that it could advise ICAO on the matter but could not overrule the international body.

Confronted with an FAA safety determination from which

there was no adequate appeal procedure, the Air Line Pilots Association took to the advertising columns of *The New York Times* on February 24, 1966, in a direct appeal to the public. Under a two-column heading, ATTENTION AIR-LINE PASSENGERS, the association accused the Federal Aviation Agency, and the airlines as well, of trying to solve a congestion problem occurring during peak traffic periods over the ocean by spacing planes closer together. "The Airline Pilots strongly object to this," the advertisement stated. "Their experience clearly indicates that present navigational devices are totally inadequate to safely reduce the lateral separation of airliners while operating over the ocean. Flight safety is the only issue here. We, the pilots, cannot accept lower safety standards to solve the problem."

The pilots admitted that they had no legal way of blocking the FAA's order to "close up" over the North Atlantic. Instead, the pilots said the public should write or wire congressmen and senators to urge an immediate suspension of the closer separation order until such a time as the problem could be solved without increasing the risk of a midair collision. The pilots also threw in a request that the public demand an immediate investigation of the FAA's arbitrary reduction of lateral separation on the Atlantic.

The airline pilots continued their battle with the FAA into 1966. Charles H. Ruby, president of the Air Line Pilots Association, wrote FAA Administrator McKee in March, reiterating the pilots' request for public hearings on the separation standard.

The FAA countered this public campaign with a statement that the ninety-mile separation was far greater than provided virtually anywhere else in the world and that aircraft flying over the United States usually maintained a separation of only ten to twenty miles. Furthermore, a ninety-mile separation standard had been used between New York and Puerto Rico for more than two years "without derogation of safety."

The FAA also noted that the reduction had been under consideration for some time, and although the pilots had been invited to comment on the reduction several times in the previous year, they had not chosen to do so. The FAA claimed that the decision to adopt the new standard was not taken until more than 7,000 inflight observations had been made by technical experts from both government and industry.

The International Airline Navigators Council strongly urged ICAO, in March, 1966, to return to the 120-mile lateral separation standard until all airlines flying the route could demonstrate adequate navigational accuracy. The council said it would be possible to remain within the ninety-mile separation limit through the use of existing navigation aids, "provided only that the flight crew include one man qualified to use the aids and employed solely for that purpose."

In mid-March, the International Federation of Airline Pilots Associations met in Auckland, New Zealand, and adopted a recommendation that its members use a 120-mile or more lateral separation on North Atlantic flights. The federation postponed its threatened strike over the separation issue, but adopted a resolution stating that if the separation situation was not resolved to its satisfaction within three months, another meeting would be called to discuss further action. The decision required that pilot members request 120-mile lateral separations for Atlantic Ocean crossings above 29,000 feet. If this was refused, the pilots were required to file a flight plan for a transatlantic crossing below 29,000 feet—where the 120-mile separation rule still applied —even though an en route refueling stop was made necessary by the lower altitude.

At the same time, the FAA announced that it would accede to the request of the Airline Pilots Association for a public hearing on the issue. These hearings involved nearly two months of direct testimony and rebuttal, during which FAA defended Project Accordion, and the pilots attacked it. In place of the Accordion data, the pilots presented their own study of navigational accuracy on the North Atlantic. Not surprisingly, it indicated that the ability of some airlines to navigate the North Atlantic over a predetermined track was not very good. One suggestion that came out of the hearings was to establish two tracks: one for airlines that had proved they could keep within the ninety-mile separation distance and another for those whose navigation ability precluded this. It was also claimed that the 120-mile separation was a safe minimum because it had been in use ever since regularly scheduled airline flights had begun over the North Atlantic, and no inflight collision had ever occurred. In June, 1966, the FAA announced that, with the agreement of other affected governments and ICAO, the 120-mile separation would be restored, pending additional studies.

AIR SAFETY RESEARCH

Crashes do not always take place by accident. The FAA and the Flight Safety Foundation conducted a controversial and dramatic controlled crash of an obsolete DC-7 airliner in 1964. The deliberate wrecking of a worn-out airliner carrying dummy passengers was the first of a series of four tests aimed at solving one of aviation's most difficult problems— reduction of crash fatalities. Commenting on the tests, the FAA noted that "in recent years several hundred passengers have been killed in accidents they might have survived with adequate protective devices; other hundreds have perished in fires after surviving the crash." The DC-7 airliner used in the 1964 test was purchased by the FAA from an airline salvage company. The locale for the test was Deer Valley Airport, Arizona, just north of Phoenix. The aircraft carried sixteen dummy passengers and twelve cameras, in addition to an elaborate set of instruments to record the impact forces in the passenger cabin and the stress on the airframe and component systems. The plane's engines were started, and the aircraft was sent down a runway and accelerated to a speed of 160 miles per hour just before it crashed into a prepared barrier. Preliminary results indicated that live passengers, using the same protective devices as the dummies, would have survived in most cases.

As a result of press inquiries and television requests for coverage, the crash tests received widespread public attention. This caused the airlines to be both publicly and privately critical of FAA "sensationalism." Perhaps as a result of this criticism, the FAA did all it could to soft pedal a later but similar test, which utilized an old Lockheed Constellation.

During fiscal 1964, the FAA also stepped up its experimental testing of techniques for suppressing fires following a crash, and continued its investigations of inflight structural failures. One project concerned the stability of aircraft structures after bird strikes. Another series of tests, conducted by NASA at the FAA's request, was intended to identify structural failures in accidents involving light aircraft. The type of accident studied involved structural failure during recovery from a high-speed dive after the pilot has lost control of the aircraft. A system augmenting the stability of light aircraft was installed in a Beech Debonaire to determine what value it might have in preventing initial loss of control.

Early in 1965, the FAA amended its rules on evacuation of aircraft to require that all carriers and commercial operators using aircraft with a seating capacity of more than forty-four passengers demonstrate, among other things, the ability under simulated emergency conditions to evacuate a full passenger load through only half of the plane's exits within a two-minute period. In addition, such planes must be equipped with better emergency lighting and larger emergency exit signs. They must also have ropes (or approved similar devices) over wing exits, and battery-powered megaphones. Under the new rule, each crew member must be assigned to specific emergency evacuation duties. The number of flight attendants must conform to a standard based on the seating capacity of the plane, and passengers must be briefed on the location of all emergency exits and be furnished cards showing their operation.

During fiscal 1965, as part of its program to improve the stopping capability of civil transport aircraft under adverse runway conditions, FAA developed and began testing a special-purpose vehicle which incorporated scientific friction measuring equipment. Specifications for appropriate firefighting equipment were also issued, and a training film on airport safety was in preparation.

FAA research does not always lead to a tightening of the rules; sometimes the research has the opposite effect. On September 30, 1965, the FAA modified its requirements which made it necessary for jet airline pilots to wear oxygen masks when flying above 35,000 feet. Under the new rules, requirement for one pilot at the controls to have the immediate use of oxygen applies only above 41,000 feet, where the time element is much more critical in the case of sudden decompression. Since airlines do not generally operate above 41,000 feet, this requirement was expected to have relatively little effect on pilots. The new rules were intended to provide relief from mask-wearing, which pilots of turbine-powered planes found uncomfortable. The FAA admitted that six and one-half years of operating experience with turbojet planes had shown that sudden decompression occurred very infrequently and was rarely serious.

Two FAA seminars on air safety and emergency evacuation held in March, 1966, brought forth a wide variety of testimony, some of it conflicting, on what is needed to make transport aircraft safer in the event of a crash. The FAA reported that demonstrations of emergency evacuation of airliners had resulted in the development of a door-mounted, inflatable cabin exit slide. These test demonstrations resulted in other improvements in design and maintenance of emergency equipment. The time required to evacuate an airplane had dropped from over three minutes, when the FAA's study was first begun, to less than one minute.

Other potential improvements in evacuation standards were under consideration, such as requiring that inflatable slides be installed at floor-level exits, mandatory stationing of cabin attendants near the exits, improvements in passenger briefing methods, and better means of identifying exits for emergency use. The FAA reported to the seminar that cabin materials in today's jet transports were the best the current state-of-the-art produces, many of the materials having self-extinguishing capability in case of fire. Nevertheless, further tests were being conducted on cabin materials, with particular attention to the smoke- and fume-producing capability of fabrics and plastics used in the cabins.

The Air Line Pilots Association submitted a seventeen-page statement to the seminar, calling for extensive modification of the interior of most transport aircraft and, in some cases, calling for more cabin attendants as well. The Transport Workers Union, in its presentation, called for federal licensing of flight attendants. "We do not subscribe to the airlines' arguments that flight attendants are pretty little luxuries," James F. Horst, the union's international executive vice-president, said. "They are professionals whose presence in the air is required by the federal air regulations as a safety measure. And we believe they should be licensed as such." Mr. Horst charged the airlines with "irresponsible neglect" of the safety of flight attendants. He pointed out that the only flight attendant that can aid in an emergency is one that is alive. The practice of having stewardesses sit on jump seats or "in washrooms or coat closets" during landing and take-off exposes them to great danger. Mr. Horst also recommended additional fire extinguishers, independent emergency power for the cabin address system, better control of carry-on baggage to eliminate blocked exits, and better inflight briefing of passengers. "Flight safety in recent years has been virtually abandoned by the airlines in their quest for a greater profit," said Mr. Horst. "We believe the time has come for a reversal of this policy—that the time has come for the FAA to take the side of the public in opposing the sacrifice of safety on the altar of profits."

One of the more dramatic moments of the 1966 seminar was the appearance of one of the survivors of the November 11, 1965, crash of a United Air Lines Boeing 727 jet at Salt Lake City—R. H. Dawson, a chemical engineer with the du Pont Company. One of his suggestions emphasized the need for a detailed pre-takeoff briefing for passengers, using a miniature mock-up to show the exact location and operation of exits. "It is better to improve the chances of survival by scaring a few people than to pay off death claims after an accident," said Mr. Dawson. He also suggested that the airlines consider adopting "tactile identification guides," such as roughened fabrics near the exits, so that the passengers could find their way out, even if the cabin was totally obscured by smoke. He criticized the small number of emergency exits, especially on jet transports with high seat density. "The exits are good on most piston aircraft," Mr. Dawson admitted, "but the seating capacity of larger aircraft should be limited to the number of persons who can be evacuated in one minute." The Salt Lake City accident was a classic example of the need for better evacuation procedures. Five of the six exits were in a six-row area. Passengers managed to open five of these six exits, after fumbling with three out of the five. More lives might have been saved if the exits had been opened faster. When Mr. Dawson finished his presentation, he was applauded by the overflow audience attending the Washington seminar.

Because of the mounting costs of the war in Viet-Nam, all government agencies were under budget pressure during 1966 and 1967. The FAA was no exception, and to do its part in keeping federal expenses for civilian purposes as low as possible, it elected to hold down research and development work. No important projects were abandoned, but few new ones were funded in the 1967–68 budget.

One continuing project, which even expanded somewhat during the 1966–67 budget period, was research into aircraft fire hazards. One part of this study involved impact testing of a series of DC-7 wing sections which were fitted out with the latest improved bladder cells. Another part of the study concerned itself with the combustible characteristics of cabin interior materials. As part of the fire study, the FAA ran a series of tests of jelled fuels. Because the jelled fuels are semi-liquid, they must be forced out of storage tanks under pressure, but the jet engines tested ran as well with the jelled fuel mixture as with straight kerosene or standard jet fuels.

Noise suppression projects were also actively continued; a total of eighteen such projects were active as of September 30, 1966. One of the more interesting programs of research at FAA was concerned with the use of cockpit instruments to reduce training time for noninstrument rated pilots who are seeking to acquire instrument proficiency. By taking advantage of the latest types of instrumentation, the FAA discovered that the time needed to train a student to instrument proficiency—as determined by an FAA flight inspector—could be cut in half. A control group needed 55.4 hours (49.3 in a simulator and 6.1 in a typical general aviation aircraft) to obtain the skill needed to pass the FAA instrument flight rule tests. This was about average for the country. Through the use of the most up-to-date cockpit instrumentation, this time was cut to an average of 25 hours (18.5 hours in a simulator and 6.5 hours in an airplane).

Research into lightning strikes was also continued. As part of this study, an Air Force jet flew regular missions of thunderstorm penetration out of Patrick Air Force Base in Florida during August, 1966. A total of seventeen lightning strikes were triggered, and excellent photographic records were made of the strikes. Some of these photographs were thought to be the first close-ups of actual lightning. The lightning hazard of fuel vents was also under study. It was found that the fuel fumes from wing tip vents could be ignited by a direct stroke of stimulated lightning at all wind velocities. Although ignition became more difficult at higher velocities, when ignition did occur, it resulted in more violent explosions.

Another continuing program of research involved a study of heaters in light aircraft, the relationship between heater failure and carbon monoxide poisoning, and an evaluation of low-cost carbon monoxide indicators. Ways to improve runway traction were also studied. As a result, the principal runway of the Washington National Airport was grooved in 1967 to improve its stopping characteristics during times of rain or slush.

IX

Airports and Airport Aid

Each year, the FAA prepares the National Airport Plan, which forecasts for the next five years the requirements for an adequate system of airports. To qualify for federal assistance, a community must be listed in the National Airport Plan. Congress has provided approximately $75 million in federal funds annually for grants under the program. For eligible items of airport development, airport sponsors provide 50 per cent of the cost, and the federal government matches the amount. Federal funds are made available for land acquisition as well as for the construction of runways, taxiways, parking aprons, runway lighting, and buildings for housing firefighting equipment. FAA also provides local airport projects with engineering advice and planning assistance.

If an airport can be defined as any landing strip equipped with a wind sock, the fifty U.S. states have upwards of 10,000 airports capable of accommodating airplanes, gliders, balloons, and amphibians, as well as vertical-lift aircraft. These range in size from 10,000-acre Dulles International Airport outside of Washington, D.C., to the helicopter pad on top of the Pan Am Building in New York City.

For long-range planning purposes, the FAA has included 4,100 existing and yet-to-be-built landing areas in its National Airport Plan. About 800 of these are airports still in the planning stage. Although most airports are municipal enterprises, nearly 5,000 are privately owned. These private landing fields are not eligible for financial aid under present government policies. Even so, the FAA has included about 400 private airports in its plan, either because they are airports important to the commercial air transport system or because there is a chance of the airport eventually "going public." All airports designated by the Civil Aeronautics Board for scheduled airline service under a certificate of public convenience and necessity are included in the federal plan.

Many privately owned airports on city outskirts are falling victim to real-estate promoters, hungry for undeveloped, close-in land. Because of the rapid expansion of all types of aviation, there is a growing need for more airports, and most airports in the national plan are in need of some kind of improvement. The cost of all needed improvements was estimated in 1966 at well over $1 billion.

The National Airport Plan concerns itself primarily with civil aviation, since virtually all of the needs of the Air Force can be supplied by existing military bases. In fact, with increasing frequency, military airports are being declared surplus. In 1964, for example, the Department of Defense announced discontinuance, reduction, or consolidation of military aviation activities at some ninety-five bases. Typical of these was Bolling Field, which lies just across the Potomac River from Washington National Airport, in Washington, D.C. In this case, the overlapping landing patterns of the two airports constituted an air safety hazard. When the Air Force agreed to abandon flight operations at Bolling, a civic battle immediately began over whether it would be better to centralize all private and business flying at Bolling Field and ban all general aviation activities from Washington National, or whether the land could be better used for some public works project. Suggestions for use of the airport ranged from making a public park out of it to selling it to private developers for high-rise apartment use.

In late 1965, the airport was dedicated to family unit housing for Department of Defense personnel. First commissioned as an Army Air Service field in 1917, Bolling's 905 acres will be occupied by 300 family housing units for married Navy and Air Force noncommissioned officers. The housing project is expected to cost $4.7 million.

An indication of what this means to general aviation in the Washington area can be seen by the fact that parking space for private and business aircraft is at a premium at Washington National. At peak hours, it is sometimes necessary for private planes to go to another field in the Washington area, such as Dulles International, after unloading passengers, because there is no space available for aircraft parking.

Although some cities still don't appreciate the fact, airports are a vital link in the chain of communication. Communication has always been the key to a city's growth. At one time, all of the great cities of the world were seaports. When the railroads pushed their way westward in this country, cities were born and cities died, depending on the location of the right-of-way. Today cities compete for trade and tourism by offering better airports, bigger airports, and even, in the international field, customs "free port" airports, where goods may be landed and trans-shipped without payment of duty or other local taxes. Within the fifty states, all airports are "free" of import customs duties, though landing fees are collected, of course, so competition is generally confined to the offering of improved facilities.

While much airport growth has been haphazard and unplanned, the FAA has attempted through its National Airport Plan to channel federal support as well as federal funds in an orderly way. To receive federal assistance for airport development or improvements, the owner must agree to use, operate, maintain, and improve the airport in accordance with the guidelines established by the government.

FAA is responsible for assuring compliance with government-sponsored agreements at nearly 2,000 public airports, including almost all of the country's larger air terminals. In 1965, FAA revised its compliance directives to include references to the Civil Rights Act of 1964. The revision specifies that the use and operation of the airport, including leases of premises, or agreements granting rights to offer nonaeronautical services to the public, must include the assurance required by the Act. Compliance with this requirement was incorporated into the agency's airport inspection procedures.

In addition to providing the leadership for planning and development of the national airport system, FAA operates and maintains both Washington National and Dulles International Airports. These are discussed in the next chapter. A part of the FAA's National Aviation Facilities Experimental Center, the Atlantic City Field, which is equipped with the latest navigation and landing aids, also serves as a municipal airport for Atlantic City, New Jersey. In the Pacific region, the agency during fiscal 1965 also operated Wake Island Airport. Responsibility for Canton Island Airport was turned over to the National Aeronautics and Space Administration during fiscal 1965. In Alaska, seven airports remained under FAA management at the end of the fiscal year. At the request of the Office of Emergency Planning, FAA helped to rehabilitate eight Alaskan airfields damaged by the March, 1964, earthquake.

One indication of the growing pressure on the airport system is FAA's prediction that between 1965 and 1975 the general aviation fleet of aircraft will have increased from about 96,000 planes to 160,000. These figures have been challenged by the Aircraft Owners and Pilots Association as too conservative. The association's own estimates are in excess of 100,000 aircraft for 1965 and 185,000 for 1975. Because of improved pilot training and the increased sophistication of general aviation aircraft, the private and business use of planes is expected to almost double.

Airport Lighting and Landing Aids

Federal interest in landing sites dates back to February 4, 1929, when an Airport Section was established in the Aeronautics Branch of the Department of Commerce. Principal duty of this section, which was staffed by five airport special-. ists, was to assist municipalities and other localities in selecting airport sites and to advise on proper construction methods. The first instruments-only landing was made this same year, when James H. Doolittle landed his plane without the aid of outside visual references, using a system developed by the National Bureau of Standards of the Department of Commerce. He was given directional guidance from a radio range course aligned with the airport runway, and his incoming distance to the point of touchdown was determined by radio markers. He controlled his airplane's altitude with the aid of a sensitive altimeter, a directional gyro, and an artificial horizon.

It was thirty years before the federal government finally got around to adopting standards for runway approach lighting, all-important if pilots are to be able to utilize fully the runway marker lights for landings in poor visibility. In September, 1960, after several years of study, the FAA adopted the British visual glide slope indicator system as a national standard for use by U.S. airports. Developed by the Royal Aircraft Establishment in England, the system is entirely visual and requires no equipment of any kind in the aircraft. Using varicolored lights, the system reduces the possibility that an aircraft will overshoot or undershoot the runway.

Ample airport lighting is of continuing concern to FAA.

In 1962, after many years of research, the agency adopted a new technical specification for lighting airport runway centerlines and touchdown zones. Such lights provide incoming pilots with a ground reference to enable them to judge their direction, roll, and pitch during approach and landing. The same lights provide departing pilots with directional guidance during take-off. The new standardized airport runway lights, particularly the touchdown zone lights, eliminate the so-called black hole, experienced by pilots as they transit from approach lights to first contact with the runway.

Housewives who complain about the short life of light bulbs will be interested in a new FAA approach-light lamp, based on the iodine cycle principle. The new lamp has a tungsten light source, which evaporates off the filament when the lamp is lit and condenses on the glass housing. The cycle is completed when the tungsten evaporates from the housing and returns to the filament. Besides making the filament, and therefore the lamp, last much longer than it otherwise would, this cycling process prevents the inner-surface of the lamp from blackening. The gain in lamp life is approximately sixfold. The old approach-light lamps had a life of about eighty hours. New ones still function normally after test operation at maximum intensity for 465 hours. Cost of the new lamps is only about two and one-half times that of the old.

Following the East Coast electric power blackout, which occurred late in 1965, the FAA moved quickly to designate fifty "continuous-power airports" and to supply these with emergency electric power generating equipment so they could continue in operation, even if there was another complete external power source failure. The FAA will bear the entire installation cost of the stand-by power for federally owned and operated facilities, such as control towers, airport surveillance radar, approach lights, and instrument landing systems. The FAA also decided to make funds available on a matching basis under the federal-aid-to-airports program to help local authorities finance the cost of permanent emergency power units for runway and taxiway lights owned or operated by the municipalities or the local airport operator. The fifty continuous-power airports include virtually every major metropolitan airport in the country. Since these airports generally are not more than 200 miles apart, they provide almost complete coverage for the continental United States.

One airport improvement program in particular has generated important benefits for both the traveling public and the airlines. This is the effort by both FAA and the large airport operators to make it possible for even the largest transports to land on schedule, no matter what the weather.

Early in 1967 the FAA announced that nineteen airports would be equipped for Category II all-weather landing operations, in addition to the four airports previously equipped —Dulles International, Oakland, Pittsburgh, and Denver. Category II landings are those in which the pilot is able to see the runway when his plane is 100 feet or more above the landing area and his forward visibility is at least 1,200 feet. The horizontal visibility is measured by a photoelectric device located next to the approximate point of touchdown on the all-weather runway. This device measures the horizontal visibility in terms of what is known as runway visual range (RVR). The instrument is read on a dial in the airport control tower, and the pilot coming in for an instrument landing is kept advised of the runway visual range at all times. If, in the pilot's judgment, there is not sufficient visibility so that he can adequately see the runway when he is 100 feet or more above it, or if the runway visual range drops to below 1,200 feet, the rules require that the landing attempt be abandoned and the pilot either hold near the airport for an improvement in the weather or proceed to his alternate airport. In order to qualify for Category II minimum landing rules, airports must have, in addition to the standard instrument landing system equipment, high-intensity approach lights with sequenced flashers, high-intensity runway edge-lighting, lighting of both the touchdown zone and the centerline of the runway, and all other appropriate runway markings.

Airports scheduled to be equipped with Category II facilities in 1967 and 1968 are those at Anchorage, Alaska; Atlanta, Georgia; Buffalo, New York; Chicago; Denver; Detroit; Houston; La Guardia Airport, New York; Kennedy Airport, New York; Los Angeles International; Louisville, Kentucky; Milwaukee; Newark Airport, New Jersey; New Orleans; Philadelphia; Rochester; San Francisco; Seattle, Washington; Washington National; and Bradley Field at Windsor Locks, Connecticut. Except for the airports at Philadelphia, Anchorage, and Newark, all the airports were scheduled to be certified for Category II landings by late 1967. Early in 1967, the FAA also reported that four airlines were equipping their fleet and training their flight crews in use of special airborne equipment and procedures for Category II operations.

NOISE AND OTHER AIRPORT PROBLEMS

The FAA, in its annual report to Congress for 1960, stated that "the introduction of commercial jet operations at many more of the country's airports during 1960, coupled with a greater volume of operations at major air terminals, has posed an aircraft noise problem second only to safety in importance to aviation." In recognition of the seriousness of the problem, the agency had "conducted an aggressive noise abatement program through prescribing the use of preferential runways, special arrival and departure routes, minimum latitudes, and revision of certain air traffic rules." The agency also published a guide for municipal planners, *Noise Abatement Procedures*, which recommended that land areas lying immediately under the take-off and landing patterns of jet runways be utilized for industrial, commercial, agricultural, or recreational purposes, and that the construction of residential subdivisions, schools, churches, hospitals, and other public buildings in the vicinity of large airports be discouraged.

During 1960, the FAA participated in many conferences held to find possible solutions to the noise problem. Federal policy was formulated for the financing of housing near airports. The FAA worked closely with the aviation industry's National Aircraft and Noise Abatement Council. One of the council's accomplishments was the removal of carrier-jet training operations from "noise-sensitive areas" to outlying airports, thus reducing jet traffic at busy terminals to some extent.

By 1962, the FAA had become sufficiently concerned over rising public complaints about the noise levels of the new jet transports to institute a broad noise abatement program. It established air traffic patterns and approach and take-off procedures at a number of airports to minimize community annoyance, taking advantage, whenever possible, of overwater routes, industrial complexes, and sparsely populated areas. Typical of the agency's efforts in this direction was the establishment of a revised preferential runway at Idlewild (Kennedy) Airport to relieve the concentration of aircraft arriving over communities northeast of the airport and to make greater use of Jamaica Bay for departure. Visual approach glide-slope indicators were installed at Idlewild to enable pilots to avoid lower than normal flight altitudes on landing approach. Also, during 1962, the Federal Housing Administration and the Veterans Administration launched a program to discourage residential development in high-noise-level areas adjacent to airports.

In March, 1962, the Supreme Court handed down a decision, in *Griggs* v. *Allegheny County,* that held airport operators, and not the federal government, liable for property damage caused by aircraft noise. As a consequence, no noise suits were filed against the government during fiscal 1963, but a large number of suits were filed against airports throughout the United States.

The FAA, in its 1963 annual report to Congress, claimed that it was attacking the noise problem from three fronts: (1) by reducing the noise at the source—the engine, (2) by moving the noise away from the people, and (3) by keeping people away from the noise. There were limits, however, to how far the agency could go, because of the primary requirements of air safety. Early in 1967, the FAA asked Congress for authority to impose noise-level limitations on aircraft engines as a condition of certification.

Some communities, in an effort to keep the noise away from the people, took legal steps to penalize pilots of aircraft that came too close or made much noise. The town of Hempstead, New York, for example, passed an ordinance imposing fines on pilots or companies responsible for aircraft that violated the noise-level ordinance. The FAA contested this local ordinance in court, with the support of the airlines, the Air Line Pilots Association, and the Port of New York Authority, and won the case.

In March, 1966, the White House released a report, "Alleviation of Jet Aircraft Noise Near Airports," by Donald F. Hornig, science adviser to the President, which stated that a study of the jet noise problem at the New York, Chicago, and Los Angeles airports was urgently needed. Next, the noise problem should be studied at the twenty or so major airports elsewhere in the United States, and, as soon as possible, the study should be enlarged to include all U.S. airports where jet service was expected to be offered by 1975. FAA's role in the proposed program would be to make a detailed technical study of the safety problems involved in landing approach procedures adopted to minimize noise and to explore the feasibility of climb-out procedures to determine optimum noise reduction techniques consistent with safe operation of aircraft.

Air traffic delays in terminal areas constitute another growing problem. There are two broad classes of delays: delays due to airport surface inadequacies, such as an insufficient number of runways, taxiways, run-up pads, ramp areas, and gate spaces to handle the volume of traffic; and delays due to air traffic control procedures, including those that result from a wait for clearance instructions for flight instrument rule departure and approach, those that result from maintaining holding patterns or holding at fixed locations, and those involving use of instrument flight rule departure paths that slow the flow of traffic. A 1963 study sponsored by the FAA with the cooperation of the Air Transport Association, found that airline delays were due largely to congestion on the surface of airports during the late afternoon rush hour. About one in five flights were delayed, the study found; most significant delays were concentrated at a relatively few large hub-airports.

In December, 1962, FAA took steps to reduce arrival delays at Chicago's O'Hare International Airport, at that time the busiest of all U.S. air terminals. To minimize delays pilots were permitted to make parallel instrument landing system approaches to the airport's dual runways. Approval of dual instrument approaches was given only after extensive testing under both simulated and actual conditions. Partly because of experience gained as a result of the new procedures, the FAA was able to reduce the limitations on the instrument landing runways. At first, a cloud ceiling of at least 900 feet and visibility of three miles were required. These minimums were reduced in February, 1963, to a 500-foot ceiling and two-mile visibility. In March, these figures were further reduced to 400 feet and one mile. The parallel instrument landing system of approaches and landing are used only when traffic back-up warrants. FAA's tower supervisor decides when the traffic back-up is such as to make it advisable to use the parallel runways. To speed up instrument landings, pilots must operate under instrument flight rules regardless of the weather, and their aircraft must carry communications and navigation equipment for making accurate approaches to the assigned runway. Each aircraft is radar-directed by the FAA approach control from four outer fixed points. Experience at O'Hare has provided a basis for establishing these procedures at other airports that have parallel runways, with centerlines 5,000 feet or more apart, and the prescribed air navigation facilities.

One factor retarding airport growth is the high cost of land, and the difficulties experienced by municipal authorities in obtaining land and raising the money to pay for it. In 1966 the research firm of Arthur D. Little Inc. released a study showing that more than a 100 square miles of land, with an estimated cost of more than $75 million, will be needed for the planned expansion of present airports and the establishment of new ones in approximately sixty U.S. metropolitan areas during the 1965–75 decade. Expansion of existing airports will require about $25 million, the establishment of new airports will account for about one half of this amount, and facilities to accommodate the growth in general aviation will account for the balance. Because the cost of land near airports has been rising at an annual rate of from 7 to 30 per cent, the study recommended that municipalities initiate programs to purchase airport sites in advance, as many municipalities now purchase school sites to meet future school building needs.

According to the study, New York will require 16,000 acres at a cost of $750 an acre, or a total cost of $12 million; Louisville will need a 15,000-acre airport at a cost of some $7.5 million; and New Orleans will need 4,000 acres at a total cost of $3 million. Since communities are not always able to buy airport sites in advance of their needs, the Little study recommends several ways in which the federal government might be of help. The government might purchase sites for major airports and transfer them to the airport development authorities when the airports are ready for construction, This would involve the federal government in all the problems associated with holding local land not immediately usable. Another possibility is for the federal government to increase its grant-in-aid programs for land. Instead of 50 per cent, the government might pay as much as 90 per cent of land acquisition costs. Municipal zoning for airports "seems to have been overrated," according to the Little study. A more effective way of controlling land use would be to plan in advance the total airport complex. Cargo handling facilities and industrial activities which can bear high noise levels should be located in high-noise parts of the complex. Through leasing and other arrangements, some of the land that is needed for future expansion could be turned to profitable use, and yield taxes as well. Easements might also be acquired over adjacent property such as the land beneath future approach zones, which would be subject to high noise levels.

THE NATIONAL AIRPORT PLAN, 1966–70

The first Federal Aid to Airports Act was passed on May 13, 1946; the Civil Aeronautics Administration (CAA) established forty-four district offices to administer the Act. At the same time, the National Association of State Aviation Officials approved the CAA's revised draft of the 1944 Model Municipal Airport Act, which was intended to promote uniform state legislation to enable cities, towns, and other political subdivisions to build and operate airports and to obtain aid under the Federal Aid to Airports Act. In January, 1947, regulations under the Act received final approval, and the 1947 construction program was announced; 800 airports were eligible for either construction or improvement work. The first National Airport Plan contained a three-year forecast of requirements for 4,431 airports. Twin Falls, Idaho was the first city to receive a federal grant—$384,000 of the total airport cost of $647,000.

Late in 1958, the CAA, soon to be absorbed into the FAA, announced that airports were to be considered eligible for matching federal funds on a basis of the actual or potential aeronautical needs of the community rather than, as previously, on the basis of the level of airport activity. Minimum annual activity requirements had been set at 3,000 enplaning passengers, or thirty regularly based aircraft. Under the new policy, terminal and other airport buildings (except hangars) that were necessary to serve the public were considered eligible for federal aid. Federal funds could even be used to help pay the cost of automobile parking areas for users of the airport.

This liberal policy was promptly changed by FAA Administrator Quesada in January, 1959, when he submitted to Congress draft legislation to extend the Federal Aid to Airports Act to June 30, 1963, and to authorize a total of $200 million for the four-year period. The legislation was also intended to accomplish "an orderly withdrawal" of the federal government from the airport grant program. Quesada proposed to limit grants under the Act to construction of landing area facilities, such as runways, taxiways, aircraft ramps, control towers, and lighting installations. Although there were some who questioned the new policy, Congress in the end approved it.

It isn't just FAA administrators who have strong ideas about the FAA's airport policy. In some cases so do Presidents. President Johnson, for example, believes that federal funds are best employed to promote interstate commerce. This philosophy, as developed and expanded by the Bureau of the Budget, has also had its impact on the FAA airports program. The bureau believes that major hub-airports, with their frequent interstate air carrier flights, should be given favored consideration in the allocation of funds. At the same time, less money need be spent for the smaller general aviation and noncommercial airfields. In his 1966–1967 budget presentation, President Johnson said it might be necessary to take back a third of the $75 million voted by Congress a year earlier for airport construction assistance.

Even as the FAA was revealing plans for the one-third cut in federal spending for the national airport improvement program, the agency was releasing its new five-year National Airport Plan for 1966–70, which recommended construction of 887 new landing facilities and improvements to 3,219 others at an estimated cost of $1.28 billion. New facilities proposed by the plan include 762 airports, 124 heliports, and one seaplane base in Alaska. Basis for the new five-year plan was a predicted rise in the number of domestic air carrier passengers from 82.5 million in fiscal 1965 to 107 million in fiscal 1970. The FAA also predicted a sharp rise in the flight time of general aviation aircraft. In 1965, general aviation's flight hours totaled 16.3 million. This figure was expected to increase to 19.5 million by 1970.

Approximately $1 billion dollars will be needed for airport improvements during the five-year period, plus $300 million more for construction of 887 new landing facilities. The National Airport Plan, however, does not commit federal funds, but merely blueprints the future needs of the nation for an adequate system of airports.

When the FAA administrator sent the Federal Aid to Airports Bill to Congress early in March, 1966, the earlier demand by the President for a cutback in fiscal 1967 funds had apparently not been included. The proposed legislation, as finally delivered to Congress, continued the federal-aid-to-airports program for three more years at the same level—$75 million a year.*

The fact that the program authorization was kept at the same annual level was interpreted by some of those who fought for restoration of the cut as a victory. In fact, the program was simply an authorization request, which must be followed up each year by a specific request for appropriations. Any time the White House wants to, it can cut the program back by the simple device of not committing the money that it does not want to spend. The Department of Defense has taken this step on a number of occasions by refusing to spend money that Congress insisted was needed to keep a program going—such as the manned bomber program.

As early as 1964, President Johnson gave warning that he intended to spend most federal airport funds on airports which serve a significant volume of commercial air traffic. At a budget briefing for the press in January, 1964, Administrator Halaby said that this change of philosophy reflected the Budget Bureau's belief that "general aviation is fairly well off financially, its other resources are adequate, and it involves a relatively small number of people." At that time, there was no indication that the level of spending would be cut, but it was likely that neither the President nor the Bureau of the Budget was aware of the economy measures that might have to be taken as a result of the war in Viet-Nam.

As already noted, one of the first actions of FAA's first administrator was to ask Congress to phase out the federal-aid-to-airports program entirely, thus reflecting a feeling widely held that airports should be financed locally, since

*The Viet-Nam conflict has had only a minimal effect on the airport aid program. In the 1967–68 budget presentation, the program was scheduled to continue at close to the $75 million level, except that $10 million had been withheld from the 1966–67 project commitments. This sum was not being returned to the Treasury by the FAA but would simply "be carried forward" until such a time as the war costs were down to a point where civilian programs could again be supported fully.

they are basically local assets. There has also been criticism of the program from time to time on the grounds that too much of the money goes to municipalities that could well afford airport improvements without federal aid.

The Aircraft Owners and Pilots Association (AOPA), for example, has repeatedly criticized the program because of its emphasis on major hub-airports. In an editorial in the January, 1966, *AOPA Pilot,* the association noted that since 1947 taxpayers have invested $862 million in federal funds to support airport expansion. Local and state authorities have contributed another $885 million since 1947. This makes a grand total of more than $1.6 billion invested in airports during the eighteen-year period. The *AOPA Pilot* called it an abuse of federal money to continue "showering millions of dollars of public pump-priming funds into the coffers of airports that long since have achieved minimum standards and met basic needs."

X

National Capital Airports

When FAA was established in 1958 as an independent agency, it was responsible not only for the operation of Washington National Airport in nearby Arlington, Virginia, but also for the construction of Dulles International Airport. FAA Administrator Quesada, in his previous role as aviation adviser to the President, had personally selected the Chantilly, Virginia, site for Dulles Airport, twenty-six miles west of the nation's capital, so he was familiar with the plans and hopes for the new international jet port. The origin of Dulles Airport can be traced back to September, 1950, when Public Law 762 was passed and signed by President Harry Truman, directing the Secretary of Commerce "to construct, operate, improve and maintain within or in the vicinity of the District of Columbia" a second public airport. The act authorized appropriations not to exceed $14 million for this purpose. By the end of 1951, more than 1,000 of the required 4,520 acres to build the airport had been purchased at Burke, Virginia. But local opposition quickly built up, and Congress balked at approving additional funds for the Burke site.

The Civil Aeronautics Administration, in December, 1955, following midsummer Senate hearings on the second public airport for Washington, repeated its earlier opinion that, while the Maryland site of Andrews Air Force Base was the best location for the airport, Burke, Virginia, was the best alternative. A request for $34.7 million in additional funds to complete Burke Airport was rejected by Congress when opposition to that site continued to grow. Finally, in August, 1957, Congress appropriated $12.5 million for the second Washington airport but specified that no part of this money could be spent until President Eisenhower had formally and publicly decided on a new site.

DULLES INTERNATIONAL AIRPORT

In January, 1958, President Eisenhower sent to Congress the recommendation of his special assistant for aviation, E. R. Quesada, that the second public airport be built at Chantilly, Virginia, and land purchases began the same month.

In May, 1959, FAA established a Bureau of National Capital Airports to provide basic management both for Washington National Airport and what was then called Washington International Airport. Establishment of the new bureau was originally intended to be an interim measure, pending enactment of legislation (still under consideration, at this writing) to set up a separate government corporation within the framework of FAA to handle management and operational functions at both airports. In July, President Eisenhower signed an executive order designating the airport under construction at Chantilly as Dulles International Airport, in memory of the late Secretary of State, John Foster Dulles.

By the end of 1959, the major items required for the new airport were under contract, with the exception of the terminal building and the associated public facilities. Site preparation was nearly complete and the primary portions of the runways were paved. In addition, a dramatic new concept of moving passengers from the terminal building to waiting planes was under development. This was the use of twenty giant-sized mobile arrival and departure lounges designed both to reduce the size of the terminal building and to enhance passenger comfort.

By 1962, FAA was almost ready to open its new international airport—the first airport wholly designed for the jet age. In its report to Congress for 1962, FAA expressed hopes that Dulles would provide "a fittingly impressive gateway to the seat of American government, and . . . establish the standard by which jet airports of the future will be measured." The boldly conceived terminal building, designed by the late Eero Saarinen, combined what the architect called "the excitement of travel and the stateliness of belonging to the Federal Capital."

One of the unusual features of the airport, of course, was the use of the mobile lounges. "An integral part of the total airport concept, these mobile lounges," continued the report, "remove from the terminal building area, along with aircraft servicing, the danger of fire and nuisance of noise and blast. Besides contributing to the safety and convenience of passengers, eliminating long fingers, and permitting ready expansion to meet future needs, use of the mobile lounge will reduce aircraft taxiing requirements, resulting in savings to the airlines using the airport." In 1962, the FAA negotiated a contract for the construction and operation of a 250-room hotel to be located on the airport, half a mile north of the terminal building. Because of the light traffic forecast during the early years of Dulles Airport, however, negotiations with hotel operators were not completed until 1967.

On November 17, 1962, President Kennedy formally opened Dulles International Airport. The special ceremonies attracted thousands of visitors, including foreign officials and dignitaries. Scheduled services began two days after the opening. Within six months, air carrier operations totaled seventy-two arrivals and departures daily. During its first complete fiscal year after opening, Dulles Airport handled a total of 111,071 aircraft operations. Air carriers operated a total of 28,167 flights. Operations by general aviation aircraft totaled 35,677, while military aircraft accounted for 47,227 operations. The mobile lounges had been well received by the traveling public. During fiscal 1964, these unique vehicles made more than 27,000 trips, carrying more than 700,000 passengers between aircraft and terminal.

The number of visitors who came simply to look at the airport was approximately double the number of air travelers. After less than eight months of operation, more than 750,000 visitors from all parts of the United States and the world had come to see this magnificent new air terminal facility.

In November, 1963, the FAA commemorated its own fifth birthday as well as the first anniversary of the opening of Dulles. Two days of festivities attracted more than 110,000 persons. In the following spring and early summer, about 200 persons came to Dulles each weekend to take airborne sightseeing trips, and about 400 came to ride in the mobile lounges.

Served by direct flights to Europe and by connecting flights to the Near and Far East, Dulles Airport gained steadily in air carrier traffic, airmail, and air freight. Passenger traffic during the second year of operation increased 22 per cent, as the airport played host to a total of 863,435 passengers. The volume of air cargo climbed from 14 to almost 20 million pounds. Beginning in February, 1965, aviation fuel was delivered by pipeline from refineries in Texas and Louisiana directly to Dulles' 5-million-gallon tank farm. Fiscal 1965 also saw the completion of an air cargo building and an express facility designed to expedite handling of the substantially higher volume of air cargo. In January, 1966, FAA proudly announced that Dulles had served its one-millionth passenger. Total passengers for the month topped that of the previous January by 21.2 per cent. Landings and take-offs increased by a healthy 37.4 per cent.

Even today, there are critics who call Dulles a federal

"white elephant," because it isn't operating at twice its capacity, with passenger facilities overcrowded and long waits for gate space and baggage. The airport's defenders reply that Dulles is an airport of the future and was never intended simply to be an overflow airport for the nation's capital. Others are critical of Dulles for purely provincial reasons. For example, the high-speed, no-access road which connects Dulles Airport with downtown Washington via the George Washington Memorial Parkway is looked upon by real estate developers and property owners along the right-of-way as a potential throughway to improved property values and profitable real estate dealings. Politicians, seeking favor with local voters in the area, periodically make public demands that the Federal Aviation Administration open the road to local traffic.

WASHINGTON NATIONAL AIRPORT

Dulles was not the first "model airport" for the nation's capital. In September, 1938, the CAA announced that President Franklin Roosevelt had approved its recommendation for construction of a close-in Washington national airport that would serve as a model of good airport planning for the rest of the nation. The new airport would be located at Gravelly Point, on the Potomac River, only three and one-half miles from the center of Washington, D.C. The site would include 750 acres, of which 500 would be filled land, created by dredging from the river. Construction was expected to take two years.

On June 16, 1941, Washington National Airport was officially opened. By the end of the year, almost 300,000 passengers had passed through the airport, and scheduled air carrier operations had reached a high of 192 daily. Public interest was also at a high level. By the first of December, over 2.2 million persons had visited the airport.

For the next nine years, Washington National continued to expand and prosper. Runways were enlarged, and the terminal was modernized and improved as traffic increased after the war. In 1958, the Federal Aviation Act was passed, and responsibility for Washington National passed to the FAA.

During its first year of operation under the independent Federal Aviation Agency, the airport produced revenue of $3.8 million. It ranked as third in total air carrier operations in the nation. An extensive improvement program was launched in an effort to equip Washington National to handle the rapidly increasing flow of air traffic. It was the hope of the FAA to improve the airport to a point where it could handle up to 6 million passengers a year. No mention was made of jets. The first jets to come into service—DC-8's and Boeing 707's—were too big and too heavy to use the limited-length runways at Washington National. Nobody was thinking of short-range jets in 1959. Jets were by nature long-haul aircraft. For hops of less than 1,000 miles, piston aircraft had it all over jets in efficiency. So said the experts.

By 1962, Washington National was handling nearly 5 million passengers and close to a quarter of a million carrier aircraft operations annually, making it the fourth ranking U.S. airport in terms of air carrier activity. The steady increase in passengers was expected to take a dip in 1962, when Dulles International opened, but FAA predicted that the dip would be a temporary one. Anticipating an eventual overuse of facilities at Washington National, the agency pushed ahead with its program to modernize terminal facilities and improve passenger comfort, convenience, and safety. All the concourses connecting the main terminal with the north terminal and the south finger were enclosed during 1962, providing passengers additional protection against aircraft noise and blast, as well as weather. New taxiways were constructed, and existing ones were widened.

As anticipated, fiscal 1963 was a banner year for Washington National. The number of passengers increased to an all-time record high of more than 5 million. At the same time, the number of air carrier flights declined. This paradox resulted from the fact that a greater percentage of available seats were occupied. The decrease in air carrier operations was largely offset by increased use of the airport by private and corporation-owned aircraft. The revenues generated by Washington National continued to return to the treasury an amount well over operating costs. Revenues for fiscal 1963 from all sources totaled $4.6 million. This not only provided the money necessary for operations and maintenance, but covered depreciation and interest on the capital plant and equipment, and included an excess of half a million dollars as well—which the FAA referred to in its annual report as "a comfortable margin of profit."

During 1963, a new baggage claim area was placed in service, and blast fencing was installed to protect passing autos on the adjacent George Washington Memorial Parkway. Additional parking facilities were constructed and were quickly filled to capacity by the steadily increasing flow of visitors and passengers.

Traffic again increased sharply during fiscal 1964. Passengers totaled 5.8 million, an increase of 16 per cent. Aircraft operations totaled 293,021, up 5 per cent. The failure of operations to gain in ratio with the passenger count reflected a considerably improved load factor for the airlines. The FAA reported that a new high for aircraft movements in a single twenty-four-hour period was established on November 25, 1963, the day of President Kennedy's funeral. Aircraft operations for the period totaled 1,208. Between 3 and 4 P.M. that day, there were 100 arrivals and 96 departures—more than three aircraft operations per minute.

Airport operations at Washington National had become big business. By 1965, airline ticketing amounted to more than $100 million a year. Concessionaires at Washington National grossed approximately $19 million annually. The annual payroll of all employees—government, air carriers, and concessionaires—amounted to an estimated $65 million.

The Jets Come to National

Washington National was growing on traffic brought in and out by propeller aircraft. Business jets were allowed to land, as were occasional Air Force jets—including the President's own "Air Force One"—but no airline jet transport had been allowed to land. With the advent of the French-built, twin-jet Caravelle, bought by United Air Lines for short-haul operations, pressure from the airlines to persuade the FAA to allow short-range transport jets to use Washington National began to mount. For a while, the FAA maintained stoutly that Washington National was not equipped for regular transport jet operations; to allow such planes to use Washington National was unwise, especially in view of the saturated condition of the air traffic approach zones, to say nothing of the overcrowded terminal facilities. The airlines should schedule their jets into Dulles, or, failing that, into Baltimore's Friendship Airport, which was not much farther away from downtown Washington than Dulles. Pressure from the airlines continued to build. Criticism of the FAA was reflected in trade publications and in the press.

In December, 1965, the FAA announced that G. Ward Hobbs, in charge of the two Washington airports since 1960, and before that an airline vice-president with more than twenty-five years in airline operations, would be transferred out of the Bureau of National Capital Airports. Arven H. Saunders, the bureau's deputy director, succeeded Mr. Hobbs. Mr. Saunders had had twelve years of experience in airport management, serving as airport manager at Dulles International, as well as at Raleigh-Durham and Greater

Cincinnati airports. The transfer was unrelated to the introduction of jets at National.

A month later, the FAA announced its decision to open Washington National Airport to limited short-range jet transport service. The agency was careful to explain that long-range jets would still not be permitted to operate into or out of Washington National, which would serve only the short- and medium-haul markets, while Dulles International would continue to serve the long-haul domestic and international markets. It was also explained that the airlines had agreed to limit nonstop jet operations from Washington National to a radius of approximately 650 miles, this limit to be extended as far as 1,000 miles for service that had been scheduled from the airport during 1965—meaning that medium-range jets would be able to serve Miami, Memphis, St. Louis, Chicago, Cleveland, Detroit, Minneapolis, New York, and Boston. Nonstop jets would also be allowed to fly from Washington National to Montreal and Bermuda.

Because the jets would have a higher noise level than the piston aircraft they were replacing, and to reassure local residents, particularly in the Virginia area, who had become highly sensitive to the increasing volume of aircraft noise, small and medium jets were requested to climb out of the airport area more sharply and more swiftly than propeller-driven aircraft. With this stipulation, they were allowed to use the flight pattern then in effect at Washington National.

With the intermediate jet service in operation, the FAA estimated that passenger traffic at Washington National could be expected to rise from the 1966 rate of 7 million persons per year to about 10 million within the next ten years. To accommodate this increase in traffic, the airlines planned to enlarge their facilities, and the FAA planned to further modernize the terminal facilities.

Since differences in landing fees often determine which of several close-in airports serving a metropolitan area are most used by air carriers, the FAA, at the time it announced the opening of Washington National to medium-range jets, also announced a readjustment of landing fees for jets at both Washington National and Dulles to 32 cents per 100 pounds of gross weight. Under the new schedule, net revenue from landing fees during the first year of jet operation was expected to increase by approximately half a million dollars.

BRICKBATS AND BOUQUETS

It might seem that for an agency as large as the Federal Aviation Administration, and one so well endowed with aviation experts, the operation of two civil airports would be a minor thing. But this has not proved to be so. The FAA suffers from the fact that Congress has a vital interest in Washington's airport facilities, since senators and congressmen are frequent travelers, and each traveling senator and congressman serves as a self-appointed watchdog of the national capital airports. Maryland congressmen, for example, believe that a large part of the air traffic that has long overtaxed the facilities at Washington National could well be diverted to the jet port which serves Baltimore. The FAA's efforts to switch overflow traffic from Washington National to Dulles has usually met with indignant opposition from one or more Maryland congressmen. For some unexplained reason, the Virginia congressmen whose districts include both Washington National and Dulles International have never taken an active role in the development of these two airports.

When the state of Virginia early in 1966 tentatively decided to put a 3-cent-per-gallon fuel tax on fuel pumped at all Virginia airports, FAA moved quickly. Administrator McKee, a lifetime Virginia resident, made an informal call on the state authorities in Richmond, protesting the tax, which would drive away from Dulles Airport those airlines who could conveniently shift their operations into Baltimore's Friendship Airport, where there was no state tax on fuel. As a result, Governor Mills E. Godwin, who earlier had favored the bill, withdrew his support for the tax. In testimony before the House Finance Committee at Richmond, Arven Saunders, Director of the FAA's Bureau of National Capital Airports, testified that the tax would "kill the goose that laid the golden egg" by causing the airlines to abandon Dulles Airport. Also testifying was Warren Martin, Vice-President of the Air Transport Association, who said that the tax would be higher than that imposed by any but three or four other states. Mr. Martin then produced a letter from Governor Godwin which said that while the tax was billed as one intended to promote airports—by bringing in revenues which could be spent for airport improvements—the tax might well achieve the opposite result. Following this testimony, the Virginia House Finance Committee, by a 15-to-2 vote, killed the tax proposal.

Knowing that FAA would eventually permit jets into National and thus take traffic away from Baltimore's Friendship Airport, Maryland congressmen have repeatedly tried to get Congress to pass bills taking control of both Washington National and Dulles International away from FAA. In January, 1965, for example, Maryland Representative Clarence D. Long introduced a bill to vest control of the two airports in an independent five-man board. Similar bills have been introduced with such regularity that they have become known as Friendship Airport Bills.

Senator Daniel B. Brewster (D-Maryland) was critical of the FAA's decision to allow jets into Washington National in a statement he made in the Senate on March 9, 1966. One of the leading radio stations of the Washington metropolitan area, WWDC, had commented on FAA's plans to renovate Washington National Airport, in an editorial broadcast on March 3, 1966, and Senator Brewster asked for unanimous consent to place the editorial in *The Congressional Record*. The editorial said:

> One thing you have to say for the boys at the Federal Aviation Agency—when it comes to spending money on the airports they operate, they go first-class. Back in January, the FAA announced it was, come April 24, opening National Airport to the medium-size jets. With the announcement, the point was made that no renovation of National would be required. And as for the noise of jets which some people find objectionable, FAA took a casual view. They explained that jet noise was only a little bit worse than the noise of propeller-driven aircraft.
>
> That was for openers. Now the FAA people are saying it is going to be necessary to renovate National after all—to accommodate all the traffic to be generated by the jets. The agency has a consultant's word for it that $150 million worth of renovations might be required by 1980. For a frame of reference, bear in mind the FAA's other local airport—Dulles International—cost only $108 million, complete. While local boosters hail Dulles as one of the world's beautiful air terminals, it remains, alas, relatively unused. That does not seem to trouble the FAA. When it comes to spending money on airports, they think big.

Another critic of the FAA, Wayne W. Parrish, publisher of *Aviation Daily,* said in October, 1966, in his "Personal View" column in another of his trade publications, *American Aviation,* that "in retrospect it was very unwise to have the FAA own and operate airports." He said that at the time the responsibility was given to the Civil Aeronautics Administration it seemed "logical" to have a federal agency operating Washington's principal airport as a "showcase," but Washington National was now in a crisis compounded of jets and congestion.

> There is only one sensible solution for the Washington-Baltimore area. A greater national capital airport authority needs to be created to embrace the areas of Virginia and Maryland which are contiguous to the District of Columbia. There is no sound

solution to the airport mess in the national capital except to remove airport ownership and operation from FAA to an independent tri-state authority. Among other things, general aviation critically needs new facilities, while the airline congestion at Washington National can be resolved only by an overall plan which includes rapid transit and helicopter services from a big in-town terminal connecting with Washington National, Dulles and Baltimore's Friendship Airport.

The FAA decision to let jets land at National brought forth a few bouquets as well as many brickbats. On March 22, 1966, Representative Samuel L. Devine (R-Ohio) had printed in *The Congressional Record* a letter he had written to Administrator McKee. Congressman Devine told the House that anyone with a semblance of knowledge about commercial jet aircraft could see that by the year 1970 piston aircraft would be a thing of the past in commercial operation. His brief letter to McKee said in part: "It appears to me that the complaints concerning possible noise, traffic, etc., are unrealistic and not in keeping with the times. Your decision, in my opinion, is the only proper decision that could be made in the public interest."

When Arven Saunders, in his capacity as director of the Bureau of National Capital Airports, addressed the Aero Club of Washington on March 29, 1966, he reported that Dulles International had moved up steadily from sixty-ninth place in terms of activity in 1963 to fifty-seventh place by the close of 1965. "Dulles is now operating at a rate of more than a million passengers a year and ranks forty-sixth in the U.S. in passenger traffic," Mr. Saunders told the Aero Club. He noted that the first generation jets were large, four-engine transports, well designed for long-range flights, requiring large airports, long runways—about two miles long—with much open area surrounding the runways. To meet the needs of the long-range jets, municipal airports all over the country were obliged to expand their facilities enormously. In some cases, the location of the airfield had to be changed away from the center of population because the big jets simply could not be accommodated at close-in airports, such as Washington National, with limited runways and urban surroundings.

Five years ago, it looked as though Washington's historic airport, so conveniently located at the heart of the nation's capital, had a very limited future. Today, said Mr. Saunders, the future of Washington National looks very bright. "The advent of a second generation of jets—smaller, lighter, more maneuverable, and especially designed for the short-haul market—has restored and greatly enhanced the value of Washington National to the metropolitan area." An independent economic analyst had told the FAA that the use of the new twin- and three-engine jets at Washington National would save the traveling public the equivalent of $150 million in terms of reduced travel time over the next fifteen years. The improved service and convenience would result in a very sharp rise in passenger traffic, which, according to the Washington Board of Trade, would mean 800 new jobs per year at the airport and an annual payroll increase of $7 million.

What FAA had in mind, continued Mr. Saunders, was a "reasonable and sensible" modernization program for Washington National—not a new airport. "After twenty-five years of faithful service, we believe that Washington National deserves a little face-lifting in the same way that businesses all over the area are improving and beautifying their facilities." Other cities would soon adopt the dual airport concept, he predicted. "Chicago, for example, feels confident that Midway Airport will be restored to major importance as a short-haul airport. . . . I have an idea that we are paving the way here at Washington for a much better balanced concept of airport service than now exists in many of the larger cities."

Very soon now, said Mr. Saunders, the third generation of jets—the mass transportation "air bus" transports, capable of carrying from 250 to 1,000 passengers on a single flight— would be operating. "I think that we in Washington are in a very enviable position to gain from this new development, because we have an airport capable of handling such large groups of passengers without congestion and confusion— Dulles Airport. Having both a short-haul and a long-haul airport in our area will enable us to gain the maximum advantages for the public which are offered by the aviation industry."

When the supersonic transport arrives, the advantages of this ultramodern airport will be even more appreciated. The response from civic groups in Washington to the changes at National, Mr. Saunders indicated, "had been overwhelmingly enthusiastic. Most people felt that jets would provide better, more comfortable flight service, while at the same time creating no more, and perhaps less, disturbance to people who live in the area. Our technical people are of the same opinion," he concluded. There are some private citizens, and some groups of citizens who do not share this view. They are apprehensive about an increase in the sound levels created by jet aircraft engines, especially over homes and schools. We are not ignoring these opinions. Our job is to bring about the change-over to jets with the least possible inconvenience to the public."

Mr. Saunders made an eloquent case for allowing transport jets to continue to use Washington National, as well as for allowing the FAA to continue to operate both national capital airports. But criticism of the FAA is far from silenced. The problem of jet noise from commercial transports landing and taking off at Washington National, as well as the continued lack of utilization of Dulles International, not to mention the continued agitation of senators and congressmen who would like to take all direct airport operating responsibility away from FAA and vest it in an interstate body similar to the New York Port Authority—all combine to make the FAA's Bureau of National Capital Airports the most controversial section of the entire agency.

XI

International Activities

FAA's international responsibilities range from training air traffic controllers from South America to sounding out the Soviets on navigation aid problems connected with new routes between this country and the U.S.S.R. Involvement in international activities dates back to the period immediately after World War II, when the Civil Aeronautics Administration established overseas offices in Paris, London, Cairo, Shanghai, and Mexico City, in addition to offices already established in Lima, Rio de Janeiro, and the Canal Zone. In September, 1947, CAA took over maintenance and operation of the airport facilities at the Pacific islands of Midway, Wake, and Guam, which had been operated by Pan American Airways from the time control was given up by the military.

As early as 1949, the United States and the Greek Government concluded an agreement, providing for a civil aviation mission to go to Greece under sponsorship of the Economic Cooperation Administration. Thirteen members of the CAA staff were named to the mission, which had the job of establishing, maintaining, and operating civil aviation facilities in Greece that would meet the minimum requirement for safe international air transport. The CAA team was also instructed to train Greek personnel to take over operation and maintenance of the facilities.

Fifteen years later, the air route traffic center in Athens,

Greece, was modernized by the FAA under a reimbursable contract between the U.S. and the Greek governments, totaling nearly $400,000. Equipment included one radar bright-display system, and one video mapper to be used in conjunction with the existing Athens radar system. FAA also helped install a microwave link to bring radar data into the Athens center from the radar site located some distance away. The bright-display system was the same as that used in FAA's domestic air traffic control facilities. The heart of the equipment is a cathode-ray storage tube, which converts raw radar data into a display that can be seen in ordinary lighted rooms. It also provides a "target trail history" which tells air traffic controllers not only where an airplane is but also where it has been, and the direction in which it is headed. From the blip's shape and movement, a rough estimate of speed can also be obtained.

In its first year of independent operation, FAA expanded CAA's work in the international field. Expert advisers stationed at overseas posts were increased in number from 127 to 139. An international field service division was established, and plans were made to assist the Department of State in recruiting and training aviation officers to serve as attachés in key foreign capitals, where the volume and general level of civil aviation warranted such appointments. These aviation attachés were trained by FAA to advise on aviation matters and provide a channel for exchange of aviation information between the United States and countries or areas to which they were accredited.

In addition to conducting flight inspections of facilities over certain international routes, the FAA also has responsibility for certification of airmen abroad, including airmen who are members of the American armed forces serving overseas, as well as certain foreign nationals. FAA's international personnel provide foreign flag carriers operating in and out of the United States with technical instructions and specifications governing the entry into, and through, the U.S. airspace. Such operations are monitored to ensure compliance with U.S. Federal Air Regulations.

INTERNATIONAL POLICIES

Since it was established in 1959, the FAA has maintained relationships with such international organizations as the North Atlantic Treaty Organization, the International Telecommunications Union, the World Meteorological Organization, and the International Civil Aviation Organization (ICAO). In its first year of independent operation, FAA continued the CAA policy of providing full-time services of U.S. staff members to the ICAO Air Navigation Office in Montreal, and Administrator Quesada served both as chairman of the U.S. delegation and as president of the twelfth session of the assembly of ICAO.

It was during 1959 that the FAA carried to successful conclusion a two-year effort to obtain ICAO adoption of the U.S. short-distance air navigation and distance measuring system as a world standard. This VOR-DME system (very high-frequency omnidirectional radio range, plus distance measuring equipment) was adopted by ICAO over the protests of the British delegation, which favored its own Decca navigation system. The VOR-DME system will serve as the basic short-range (200–300-mile) navigational aid standard for the world's airlines until at least 1975.

Following enactment in September, 1961, of Public Law 87-197, providing punishment for aircraft piracy and other crimes aboard civil aircraft in flight, FAA took action at the March–April 1962 meeting of the ICAO subcommittee on the legal status of aircraft, to include within the draft on "crimes convention" a provision to cover international hijacking of aircraft.

To replace the Air Coordinating Committee which President Eisenhower had abolished by executive order on October 10, 1960, the FAA took the leadership in establishing an Interagency Group on International Aviation (IGIA). The group consisted of the administrator of FAA as chairman and one representative each from the Departments of State, Defense, and Commerce and from the Civil Aeronautics Board. From time to time, members were designated by other agencies whenever the group was considering matters of substantial concern to these other agencies. The purpose of the new interagency group was to provide the Secretary of State with aviation views and recommendations on decisions affecting international aviation matters.

During 1962, for example, the Interagency Group on International Aviation dealt with more than 300 international aviation problems. Fifteen of these problems involved preparation of U.S. position papers for use in international meetings. One of the most important of these was the development of a position to be taken by the United States on the Warsaw Convention, an important but controversial international agreement on limitation of air carrier liability, to which the United States has been a party since 1934. An amendment called the "Hague Protocol" to the Warsaw Convention, which the United States was reluctant to ratify, would double the maximum permitted accidental death recovery, by insurance, under the Warsaw Convention from $8,300 to $16,600 and, in addition, would provide for the reimbursement of attorney's fees and court costs, if permitted by the local law where the accident occurred. During 1962, the interagency group conducted a thorough review of these two international agreements. The group concluded that protection of U.S. travelers was inadequate, even under the Hague amendment to the Warsaw Convention, and U.S. policy was based on this conclusion.

President Kennedy, in September, 1961, because of FAA's "concern that U.S. international air transportation policies, formulated essentially in the period near the end of World War II, might no longer adequately serve the nation's future interest," appointed an interagency steering committee to conduct a full-scale aviation policy review. Assisted by two outside groups of aviation consultants, and incorporating the views of the air carrier and aircraft manufacturers, the interagency steering committee, under the chairmanship of the FAA administrator, completed and submitted its report to President Kennedy early in 1963. In April, 1963, the President approved a statement of broad new national aviation policy based on this report. "The United States Air Transport Policy," said the President, "takes into account all U.S. interests, the health and growth of our carriers, the contributions which air transport can make to our national security, and above all, the needs of the consumer—the traveler and the shipper." The necessity of keeping the international air transport industry as free as possible from restrictions was stressed, whether these were imposed by governments or jointly agreed to by the carriers. U.S. policy should be one of free enterprise that would benefit U.S. international air carriers and strengthen the entire system generally. In accordance with the new policy, the President, on June 22, 1963, instructed the Secretary of State to organize an Inter-Agency Committee on International Aviation Policy to assist in the task of updating international aviation policy for the United States. The chairman was to be the Under Secretary of State for Political Affairs, with the FAA administrator as vice-chairman. The new policy group was to be made up essentially of members representing the same agencies as those on the Interagency Group for International Aviation, which was to continue to handle technical matters affecting international aviation affairs.

THE TECHNICAL ASSISTANCE PROGRAM

FAA's peacetime program of technical assistance to foreign countries, begun by CAA in 1949 as an experiment, has been continued and expanded. With funds supplied under the Mutual Security Act, FAA experts and advisers in a number of foreign countries supervise airport construction, installation of air navigation aids, air traffic control work, communications installation, and flight inspection facilities and techniques. In addition to serving as consultants in airport management, aviation safety matters, and aeronautical legislation, they provided advice to U.S. military aviation groups in their geographic areas. FAA personnel are also made available for temporary short-term assignments to resolve specific technical problems overseas, and there is a continuous interchange of advisory correspondence between the United States and other countries interested in obtaining U.S. views and advice on specific aviation matters. In addition, many foreign visitors come to the United States for a variety of purposes related to the advancement of civil aviation in their own countries.

The technical assistance program encourages wider adoption of U.S. techniques and enlarges markets for U.S. aeronautical products. During fiscal 1965, for instance, among the countries benefiting from FAA engineering and material services were Argentina, Brazil, Guatemala, El Salvador, Honduras, Nicaragua, Costa Rica, Lebanon, Syria, Tunisia, the United Arab Republic, Iran, Pakistan, Turkey, Indonesia, Korea, Nepal, Thailand, the Philippines, the Republic of China, and Viet-Nam. Material supplied included communications equipment, instrument landing systems, radars, flight trainers, air traffic control trainers, and instrument flight inspection aircraft. FAA specialists conducted special field studies and surveys on behalf of the State Department's

Agency for International Development (AID) in Liberia, Chad, Afghanistan, Thailand, Bolivia, Brazil, Chile, Colombia, the Dominican Republic, Ecuador, Guatemala, Panama, Paraguay, Peru, and Venezuela. By the end of the fiscal year, FAA's overseas activities connected with foreign aid included seventeen single-country civil aviation assistance groups.

In South and Central America, the Panama-based regional aviation assistance group served all of Latin America; multi-country groups served Central America from FAA headquarters in Guatemala. Staffing of these groups called for a total of 117 positions—reflecting a reduction of 11 positions during the year. Four civil aviation assistance groups—located in Brazil, Colombia, Israel, and Indonesia—completed their programs and were closed. The FAA Israel civil aviation assistance group was financed by the Israeli government; all the others were AID-financed. At the end of fiscal 1965, FAA was planning to establish assistance groups in Brazil and Bolivia, with the cost to be fully reimbursed from AID development loans to these countries. A two-man team of FAA specialists was also planned for Saudi Arabia under terms of a bilateral agreement, the cost to be reimbursed by the Saudi Arabian government.

Since the United States leads the world in the development of commercial air transportation, many of the flight and air traffic control procedures used world-wide are based on FAA models. In traffic control towers and for en route communications between aircraft and ground stations, the universal language of aviation is English. This means that an Italian pilot landing at Paris communicates with the control tower at Orly Field in English. Weather reports and other information furnished to pilots both on the ground and en route are also in the English language. Many of the air traffic controller personnel who man control towers all over the world are FAA-trained.

Candidates selected for training are sponsored either by their respective governments, by the International Cooperation Administration, or the International Civil Aviation Organization, with the initial selection being made by the trainee's own government. Such training, lasting from three to eighteen months, covers a wide range of aviation activities, such as advanced flight training, air traffic control, communications, maintenance of facilities, airplane and engine maintenance, airport management, and aviation law. Formal training is conducted at the FAA Aeronautical Center at Oklahoma City, as well as at selected universities; on-the-job training is provided under FAA auspices at government facilities, airline offices, manufacturing plants, engineering firms, and factory service schools.

The FAA's international activities have been almost completely free of criticism either by private groups or by Congress. One exception was a 1964 report, *Civil Aviation and U.S. Foreign Aid: Purposes, Pitfalls, and Problems for U.S. Policy*, prepared by Hans Heymann, Jr., for the RAND Corporation. Mr. Heymann, an economist and student of international aviation affairs, criticized what he called "showcase" projects, which often turned out to be of little real benefit to recipients. At various times, both the United States and the Soviet Union have indulged in such aid. Mr. Heymann cited as an example an international airport built by the United States "in the middle of nowhere" at Kandahar, Afghanistan, which has "no perceptible air traffic to serve." As for the Russians, the report states that eight IL-18 turbo-prop airliners were furnished to Ghana by the Soviet Union, only to be left standing virtually idle at Accra Airport "with no discernible route system to serve." The report was also critical of the U.S. decision to lend up to $20 million to Ethiopia to equip its national flag-carrier with two U.S.–built jets, and to build jet-age airports in this African country. Mr. Heymann concluded that "in a country where roads are still appalling, railroads virtually non-existent, the city drainage system embryonic, and the agriculture medieval, where cattle dung is still being collected for fuel and the population has a ninety-five percent illiteracy rate, one does not have to look far to find more economically rewarding uses for $40 million."

OCEAN AIR TRAFFIC

Under international arrangement, the U.S. is responsible for providing air traffic service affecting more than 13 million square miles of Pacific Ocean area. During 1962, the FAA took steps to improve its aviation services within this vast tract of international airspace. A contract involving more than $400,000 was let for the construction of an international flight service station and navigation aid facility on American Samoa. Work was also started on the expansion and modernization of the aeronautical telecommunications network that serves Wake, Guam, and Manila in order to permit an improved exchange of information on air movements and meteorological data.

In 1966, New Zealand became the first foreign country to sign an agreement for flight inspection of U.S. air navigation aids installed in U.S. territories in the Pacific. The agreement provides for regular inflight accuracy checks of U.S. navigational equipment serving Tafuna Airport on American Samoa. These checks had formerly required FAA aircraft to make a 5,000-mile round-trip flight from Honolulu at least three times a year at an annual cost to the U.S. Government of $33,000.

In September, 1962, the President signed Executive Order 11048, which gave legal authority for the civil administration of Wake Island to the Secretary of the Interior. The order also made effective an earlier agreement between the Department of the Interior and the FAA, under which the FAA assumed responsibility for the civil administration of Wake Island. This included the exercise of all executive, legislative, and judicial duties. The FAA, as a basis for carrying out its responsibilities, prepared and issued a new Wake Island Code, intended to strengthen the island's legal system and reduce administrative uncertainties. Civil administrators on Wake Island had formerly relied on maritime law and general criminal laws made applicable by the so-called assimilative crimes act.

Normally the FAA does not become involved in aircraft export problems, but one such problem has concerned the agency directly. During a period of several months in mid-1965, more than one hundred transatlantic ferry delivery flights were attempted in single-engine or light, twin-engine aircraft. The FAA estimated that about half these flights were involved in incidents that required either direct or indirect search and rescue assistance. This put a severe strain on Canada, but complaints were also being received from Britain, Iceland, Portugal, and other nations on the east coast of the Atlantic, since the cost of a single search and rescue mission can run as high as $85,000.

One practical solution to this problem is a guide book for pilots who are planning transatlantic ferry flights. Early in 1966, the FAA began work on such a manual. It will spell out in detail the techniques and procedures necessary for a successful North Atlantic crossing and will include complete flight plans and navigational procedures for both eastbound and westbound flights—although the primary direction of heavy traffic is east. The manual is expected to recommend that at least twelve high-frequency channels be available on aircraft radios for each flight, and at least two 60-channel, very high-frequency transmitters.

The FAA claims that most search missions are launched when a communications failure occurs. In some cases, this is no more than a lapse on the part of the pilot; in other cases it is caused by a lack of sufficient high-frequency radio capability or by improper use of the equipment available. Some troubles stem from high-frequency beams fading over the ocean. The FAA points out that there are a number of Atlantic Ocean areas where relatively short-range communication with high-frequency transmitters is at times impossible, although, at the same time, stations much farther away present no problems in communication. There are only a limited number of high-frequency channels available for communications over the North Atlantic, and there is a tendency for these to be crowded during peak airline traffic departure and arrival times.

Another major problem is weather forecasting for altitudes between sea level and 10,000 feet, where nonpressurized light aircraft usually fly. The only demand for such weather forecasts in this area is by general aviation aircraft on ferry flights. Virtually all North Atlantic weather forecasting is geared to the needs of the high-flying transport jets, which operate at altitudes of 30,000 feet or more. Weather on the North Atlantic tends to be violent, with abrupt changes. To add to the troubles of a light-plane pilot attempting an ocean crossing, weather procedures used on the North Atlantic are governed by ICAO rules and differ considerably from FAA weather procedures and terminology used in this country. Furthermore, weather conditions in general over the North Atlantic are such that light aircraft ferry operations are feasible only from mid-May to mid-September, with September a highly questionable month.

Another transatlantic crossing problem can be traced to the fact that most light aircraft being ferried across the North Atlantic are ill equipped for survival of the occupants in the case of ditching, and pilots are often not familiar with the appropriate survival techniques. The FAA guide will include both a list of equipment and suggestions for its proper use. At the same time, the guide will warn that there is small chance of survival if the pilot is forced to make a sea ditching in the North Atlantic. A 30°F surface temperature in a twenty-knot wind equals an effective surface temperature of minus 38°F. One hour's exposure in the water to this condition is almost always fatal. On the other hand, the FAA notes that nine ships are permanently stationed along trans-atlantic air routes, and these can be used both for navigation and communication relay. In case of emergency, ditching should be made near one of the ships. All are equipped to perform rescue operations.

XII

Civil-Military Cooperation

It is interesting to look back and see how the Civil Aeronautics Administration, which developed its air traffic control procedures independently, owes so much of its original authority to control air traffic to the needs of the military. It is also interesting to note that the roster of CAA officials includes so many military officers who gave their time and talent to the development of all phases of civil aeronautics over the years—not just in their work for CAA and the civilian air safety effort, but also indirectly, through advice and encouragement, to the fledgling civil transport industry.

In October, 1941, shortly before the United States became involved in World War II, the Secretary of War designated a number of domestic airports as essential to the national defense. War Department certification made it possible for the Civil Aeronautics Administration to take over operation of the control towers at these airports. This procedure had been worked out earlier in 1941 and had been incorporated into the supplemental National Defense Appropriation Act of August 25, 1941. Under this Act, either the Secretary of War or the Secretary of the Navy could certify an airport as essential to the national defense, whereupon the CAA was authorized to take over operation of the designated airport control tower, which, until this time, had been operated by the local airport authority. CAA began operating such control towers in November, 1941.

WARTIME—AND AFTER

On December 1, 1941, all pilots and all aircraft were required to have federal certificates. Previously, a lack of regulatory legislation in certain states had permitted both uncertificated pilots and uncertificated aircraft to operate so long as they stayed outside federal civil airways. On December 13, 1941, the week after Pearl Harbor, President Roosevelt directed the Secretary of Commerce to "exercise control and jurisdiction over civil aviation in accordance with requirements for the successful prosecution of the war, as may be requested by the Secretary of War." An executive order authorized the Secretary of War "to take possession of any civil aviation system or systems or any part thereof to the extent necessary to the successful prosecution of the war." A few days after this directive was issued, the Secretary of War requested that previously planned CAA projects for the establishment of air route traffic control centers, and the completion of a nation-wide traffic control teletype network "be expedited to the fullest extent possible in the interest of national defense." In response to this directive, CAA established seven new centers in the next ninety days. In April, 1942, CAA, in an effort to help meet wartime pilot requirements, increased the maximum permitted monthly number of flying hours of pilots from 85 to 100 hours. It was not until July, 1947, that the 85-hour maximum was reinstated.

In February, 1942, at the request of the War Department, the CAA increased its assistance to the Army Signal Corps, which was responsible for setting up a world-wide network of navigation aids for the use of the Air Transport Command. First priority was assigned to extending a chain of navaids to the northeast to guide the steadily increasing flow of military aircraft being ferried to Britain. Later, in anticipation of the African invasion, CAA engineers installed radio communication and air navigation facilities at nine large air bases in South America and Africa, and set up what was known as the Southeast Airway. Later, radio ranges and other facilities provided an electronic pathway to the Pacific battlefields—southwest to Australia, and north from Seattle to Attu. By the end of 1945, CAA had established navigation facilities at some 200 locations outside of the United States at a total cost of about $38 million.

In July, 1943, the CAA inaugurated its flight communications service, which enabled a pilot who called the CAA communicator by aircraft radio to obtain information about important changes in weather along his route, as well as notice of any out-of-service airway beacon that might affect the safety of the flight.

Soon after VE day, the CAA announced that its operation of airport traffic control towers in twenty-three cities would terminate, because the War Department had advised CAA that they were no longer essential to the war effort, and Army Air Force funds for their operation could no longer be furnished. At this time, CAA was operating a total of 115 control towers that had been designated by the War and Navy Departments as essential to national defense.

In the years that followed World War II, the CAA and the military operated their separate air traffic control towers on a friendly but "arm's length" basis. This worked reasonably well, even though at times a CAA controller and an Air Force controller might inadvertently assign the same envelope of airspace to a civil and a military plane. With most piston aircraft, closure rates were such that the "see and be seen" techniques of piloting worked well enough to accommodate occasional controller errors. When jets came on the scene, the picture changed. The Air Force got them first, and had the greatest number, but the airlines were not far behind, and what the airlines lacked in aircraft numbers, they made up in hours of utilization. Closure rates for two jets approaching head-on are such that when either pilot (or both) sees the situation, it is too late to take corrective action.

Everyone was aware of the jet traffic problem, but nobody wanted to talk about it. Advent of the jet age meant that the time had come for all air traffic control to be placed under a single responsible agency, however distasteful this might be to some Air Force elements. When the inevitable midair collision came, however, it was not between a military jet plane and a civil aircraft, or even between two jets. On June 30, 1956, a TWA Constellation and a United Air Lines DC-7 collided in midair at 21,000 feet over the Grand Canyon. Investigations by two House committees as well as the Senate Aviation Subcommittee, chaired by Senator A. S. Mike Monroney (D-Oklahoma) focused on the inadequacies of CAA's air traffic control procedures and indirectly brought out the fact that CAA's appropriations were niggardly and its controller's salaries absurdly low, considering the responsibilities involved. There was some airing also of the CAA-Air Force battle over standardization of air navigation aids, particularly whether civil aircraft should adapt to the military's system, or the military should change to the CAA-developed beacon system. On the basis of the hearings, with some support from the White House in the person of General Quesada, President Eisenhower's assistant for aviation affairs, a federal aviation act was under consideration in 1958 when a second midair collision occurred. This time it was an Air Force jet which collided with a United Air Lines transport. The two planes were each under the air traffic control of different agencies: CAA was guiding the transport, and an Air Force tower was controlling the jet. Airline industry support was quickly mobilized behind Senator Monroney's efforts to draft a bill to establish an independent federal air traffic control agency, one that would have control over all U.S. military and civil air traffic.

As an interim measure the Secretary of Commerce and the Secretary of Defense early in 1958 signed a joint-use agreement, which had as its objective "the avoidance of duplicating facilities, equipment, and overlapping functions; increased capability of each function and an air traffic control system functionally compatible with the nation's defense facilities in peace and war." It was agreed that the Airways Modernization Board would develop criteria for the practical application of this policy.

Then in August, 1958, the Federal Aviation Act was passed and signed, and the FAA was set up as an independent agency on the last day of December, 1958. One of the new administrator's first decisions was to make the transition from military to civilian traffic control as painless as possible for all concerned. In the late summer of 1959, Administrator Quesada announced that the agency was preparing to take over the operation of military air traffic control facilities at 337 locations around the world. Under the plan, called Project Friendship, the military functions were to be absorbed in four specific areas: (1) military flight service; (2) flight inspection of military air navigation facilities; (3) military air traffic controller training; and (4) operation of military air navigation and traffic control facilities.

In November, 1959, the Strategic Air Command began using seven special routes established by the FAA to carry out day-and-night, all-weather, low-altitude training missions. Routes for Operation Oil Burner—code name for these SAC radar bomb runs over simulated targets throughout the country—were laid out to avoid congested population and airport centers to the maximum extent possible.

Administrator Quesada told the President and Congress in his 1960 annual report that establishment of the FAA had virtually eliminated the wasteful duplication of money and effort in the research and development of air traffic management equipment. He pointed out that during 1960 FAA's scientists and engineers had begun testing the first components of a wholly new semi-automatic air traffic control system, which was being developed under the code name of

Data Processing Central. This was intended to relieve the controller of his routine functions and free him for all-important decision making.

By the end of 1960, fifty long-range radars and forty radar approach control facilities were being operated on a joint civil-military use basis. On December 15, 1960, the FAA began taking over a number of military flight service functions which were transferred in their entirety, thus releasing military personnel engaged in these tasks for other essential military duties. Radar flight advisory service for 35,000 miles of high-altitude civil air routes was made possible by the use of Air Defense Command long-range radars, operated by FAA personnel.

UNIFIED AIR TRAFFIC CONTROL

During 1962, the agency continued to make progress toward a unified air traffic control system. An FAA-authorized manual was accepted for the guidance of both military and civilian personnel who provide air traffic control services. In addition, FAA rules, as contained in Part 60 of the Civil Air Regulations, were made legally binding on both military and civilian pilots. The FAA now has basic responsibility for all research and development work relating to air traffic control functions, operations, and equipment, except where the requirements are peculiar to warfare. In its annual report for 1962, FAA said that to become a truly joint civil-military service organization, the FAA "needs a specialized work force, not only career dedicated in peacetime, but also responsive to military requirements in time of war or national defense emergencies." To provide this specialized work force a federal aviation service, basically civilian in character, but subject to being placed in military status by the President if necessary, was required. Membership in such a service should be voluntary and should include only those

FAA employees who were essential to the agency's national defense mission. Preliminary estimates indicated that this would be a substantial number. The Defense Department endorsed the plan, but a bill to establish such a program, introduced the previous September in both houses of Congress, failed to obtain affirmative action.

In the meantime, the FAA disclosed that difficulties had been encountered in transferring to FAA the numerous Department of Defense air traffic control facilities, which were scattered throughout the world. A three-agency steering group was formed, empowered to direct a thorough study of the questions involved in the transfer—particularly cost, expected benefits, operational implications, and phasing. The steering group comprised representatives of the Bureau of the Budget, the FAA, and the Department of Defense.

During fiscal 1962, however, the FAA expanded its joint military-civilian use of long-range radar facilities serving both the military and civilian traffic. These were increased from fifteen to twenty-seven, and coverage was broadened from fifteen to nineteen states (including Alaska) and Guam. Nine of the facilities belong to FAA and the remaining eighteen to the Air Defense Command of the Air Force. During the fiscal year, the FAA participated in more than sixty military exercises performed by the military. The most comprehensive of these was the North American Air Defense Command Operation Sky Shield #2. Beginning at 1 P.M. eastern daylight saving time on October 14, 1961, the exercise lasted for twelve hours, during which time special Civil Air Regulations prohibited all flying by any nonparticipating aircraft within the continental United States. This grounding of civil aircraft was necessary because of the maneuvering in large numbers of bombers and interceptors at both high and low altitudes, in both ascending and descending patterns, in one of the most realistic air defense exercises ever conducted. FAA's participation went beyond the mere clearing of the sky. For the first time, the agency's radar facilities were actively engaged in recovering military aircraft.

FAA also participated in air traffic control work for the nuclear test in the Pacific which began in February, 1962, and assisted in solving the air traffic control problems presented by an Air Force radar bomb scoring program called Oil Burner. During 1962, the Air Force expanded the Oil Burner target operations and made them semimobile, using trailer vans and even express trains.

A most realistic test of FAA-Defense cooperation occurred on October 21, 1962, the day before President Kennedy made his national broadcast about the Cuban missile crisis. FAA was requested to provide emergency air traffic control services at Key West to support possible military operations. Only five hours later, on the same day, tower services were operating from the roof of the Key West terminal building. FAA controllers remained on duty, providing uninterrupted service, while an inexpensive temporary tower was constructed around them. At the same time the FAA air route traffic control center at Miami was designated responsible for administration of special FAA Regulation 454, which went into effect October 24, prohibiting civil aircraft from flying over approximately the southern two-thirds of the State of Florida and adjacent waters without a flight plan or without functioning navigation equipment and two-way radio communication. This special regulation was relaxed in November, although Key West and the majority of the Florida Keys remained for a time in the restricted area.

In March, 1963, the interagency steering group reported to Administrator Halaby that integration of Department of Defense air traffic control and related functions into the FAA should proceed on a "go slow" basis. Instead of the general assimilation of the military air traffic control work, the absorption should take place on an individual basis in which the selection of the facility to be integrated would be agreed upon by both the FAA and Air Force. The steering group also recommended that additional work be done on programs for the joint training of traffic controllers.

Programs for the joint use of long-range radars continued during 1963. Seventeen FAA or military radars were converted to joint use, bringing the over-all total of double-duty radars to forty-four. FAA also extended its joint-use concept to telecommunication facilities. One result of this was an agreement between the FAA administrator and the Deputy Secretary of Defense, calling for world-wide consolidation of FAA-Defense operational communication service. FAA estimated that the resulting bulk tariff savings would amount to more than $6 million a year.

Participation of FAA in military training exercises produced invaluable experience for the personnel involved. FAA reported to Congress in 1964 that "participation in war training exercises frequently allowed FAA field organizations to test and perfect their own emergency readiness plans." The value of this training was given a dramatic demonstration when an earthquake struck Alaska on March 27, 1964. The previous October, the FAA had participated with the military in a six-day Alaskan exercise, one portion of which was based on the assumption that an earthquake measuring 8.0 on the Richter scale had struck. Six months later, an actual earthquake struck Alaska, registering between 8.5 and 8.7 on the scale. The lessons learned during the military exercises contributed greatly to the rapid restoration of FAA services after the disaster.

PERSONNEL AND AIRSPACE

One detail of civil-military cooperation that worked very smoothly was the integration of military officers into the FAA staff. The law that created the FAA instructed the administrator to "provide for participation of military personnel in carrying out functions relating to regulation and protection of air traffic, including provision of air navigation facilities and research and development with the respect thereto, and the allocation of airspace." Military participation was not to be limited to advisory functions. Personnel assigned to duty from the armed forces were made part of the regular staff of the agency.

Despite the sensitivity of Congress to the integration of military personnel into a civilian agency, the FAA obtained more than a hundred military officers on assignment during the first year of its existence. They were of great value to the agency in its transactions with the Department of Defense, as well as in FAA's research and development programs and its over-all planning.

Only commissioned officers were assigned, and although all the services were represented, the majority of officers were from the Air Force. During the first six and one-half years of FAA's operations, the number of officers assigned ranged from 133 the first year to 74 late in 1965. The average was less than 100, or about one military officer for every 500 civilian employees. About two-thirds of the officers have been assigned to two FAA component organizations—the Research and Development Service, which has the largest number, and the Air Traffic Service.

In May, 1959, soon after the agency was established, the FAA adopted new procedures for allocating airspace to meet the needs of both civil and military users. In keeping with the authority vested in the administrator under the Federal Aviation Act, the revised rules required that airspace be assigned in accordance with provisions of the Administrative Procedures Act, superseding the procedures under which airspace allocation problems were processed through the Air Coordinating Committee.

As of June 1, 1959, there was a total of 143,678 square miles of airspace over the United States and its territories that had been allocated as restricted. In addition to these 247 restricted military areas, there were 9 prohibited areas, totaling 5,126 square miles, which had been established by Presidential order. By the end of the year, the FAA had persuaded the military to give up 17 of its restricted areas, or a total of 9,174 square miles. At the same time, 7 new restricted areas, totaling 700 square miles, were established. Five other restricted areas were reduced in size with a saving of nearly 15,000 square miles, and one existing restricted area was increased in size by 13 square miles. The effective height of 5 restricted areas was reduced, and 3 others were reduced in terms of the number of hours per day that they were used. Net result of this initial effort was to reduce restricted airspace by a total of nearly 10,000 square miles. By 1965, 58,-000 square miles of previously restricted airspace had been made available to civil aviation.

XIII

The Supersonic Transport

One way the FAA discharges its responsibilities for the promotion of aviation is through encouragement and assistance in the development of new aircraft designs. In 1963, for example, the FAA held a design competition for a small modern air transport which would be useful to both the local service carriers and the government. In 1964, the competition ended with an FAA statement that "none of the designs submitted was considered to represent a sufficient advance in the state of the art to warrant award of a detailed design contract." The following year, FAA worked closely with the Air Force and the Lockheed Aircraft Corporation on the C-141, a giant intercontinental cargo jet. Hopeful that the C-141 would have civil as well as military application, FAA worked to improve economy of operation and other features that would make the C-141 more attractive to the airlines. Unfortunately, this effort was not too successful, and only a small number were sold for commercial operations.

THE SST PROPOSALS

By far the most important of the FAA's efforts to develop new aircraft has been its supersonic transport (SST) program. This dates back to late 1960 and early 1961 when the

FAA negotiated with the Air Force for engineering and contracting support for a supersonic transport engine design study. This study was prompted by a June, 1960, report of the House Committee on Science and Astronautics, which recommended that Congress support a government program for the development of a commercial supersonic transport. The committee also called on the administration to complete the B-70 manned bomber program, in the hope that early production of the giant bomber would "blaze a technological trail" for the SST. The committee also recommended that the National Aeronautics and Space Administration take the lead in devising an appropriate program.

In September, 1961, FAA signed an agreement with the Department of Defense and NASA, outlining a management plan for research and study of a commercial supersonic aircraft. The agreement placed responsibility for program leadership in FAA, and provided for an SST steering group, headed by the FAA administrator and composed of the Assistant Secretary of the Air Force for Materiel, and NASA's director of Advanced Research and Technology. The steering group was to devise broad policy and give over-all guidance to the program.

Congress appropriated $11 million in 1962 to FAA for directed research toward the eventual production by the United States of a 2,000-mile-an-hour transport. In utilizing the new appropriations, FAA awarded contracts to industry for exploratory research in such fields as aerodynamics, propulsion, structures, materials, fuels, and operating problems, to parallel in-house research and study by FAA, NASA, and the Department of Defense. The second year's effort was aimed at testing and evaluation of practical design factors.

On June 5, 1963, President Kennedy announced his formal decision to go forward with development of the supersonic transport. His decision followed a two-year period of government and industry feasibility research, for which Congress had appropriated some $31 million. President Kennedy proposed that the government should bear 75 per cent of the cost of development, with private industry contributing the balance. Following this announcement, the President requested, and Congress later appropriated, $60 million for the go-ahead phase. This top-level decision brought with it a change in the organization of the FAA staff assigned to the supersonic development program. The program was taken out of the Aircraft Development Service and made the responsibility of a new deputy administrator for supersonic transport development. On July 29, 1963, President Kennedy appointed a former Northwest Orient Airlines Vice-President, Gordon M. Bain, to the job. Until the appointment of Bain, responsibility for the government-industry program had been scattered among the various operating divisions of the FAA.

By this time, the first draft of a request for proposals had gone out for comment to the airlines and manufacturers as well as to other government agencies concerned. The final draft, released to the airframe and aircraft engine manufacturers on August 15, 1963, established design and performance objectives for the aircraft, engines, and associated systems. The primary objectives were:

1. Optimum operating safety and potential commercial profitability;

2. Development cost and sales price to be at the minimum practical level;

3. A range of 4,000 statute miles, or a little more than was needed for a New York to Paris flight;

4. A capacity of from 125 to 160 passengers, plus 5,000 pounds of cargo and mail;

5. The ability to operate from present-day (1963) airports without runway extensions;

6. A cruising speed of about 1,500 miles per hour (Mach 2.2) or better;

7. An airport noise level no greater than the noise level of present long-range, subsonic jet transports; and

8. Maximum sonic boom levels of two pounds per square foot overpressure during the brief period when the aircraft accelerated to supersonic speed, and 1.5 pounds per square foot during the initial aircraft cruise.

By September, 1963, three major airframe manufacturers (Boeing, Lockheed, and North American) and three major engine builders (Pratt & Whitney, General Electric, and Curtiss-Wright) had advised the FAA of their intentions to submit proposals in the design competition.

Although the program provided for government assistance to the manufacturers in order to help meet the high cost of development, the government made it clear that eventually provision would have to be made for the treasury to recapture development funds through royalties to be paid by the airlines purchasing and operating the supersonic aircraft. The deadline for submission of initial design proposals was January 15, 1964. In the meantime, the FAA announced that it would accept "shadow orders" and assign delivery priorities. First of these delivery position reservations was received on October 14, 1963. By the end of fiscal 1963, thirteen foreign and seven U.S. flag carriers, plus one U.S. aircraft-leasing company had requested a total of ninety-one delivery positions. In establishing delivery positions, primary consideration was given to the order in which the carriers submitted requests for delivery priorities, then to a sequence of market priorities based on the geographical areas served by each U.S. and foreign carrier, as follows: (1) U.S. flag carriers—Atlantic; (2) foreign flag carriers—Atlantic; (3) U.S. flag carriers—Pacific; (4) foreign flag carriers—Pacific; and (5) U.S. domestic carriers. The principal aim of this system was to make the supersonic transport available to the broadest possible international and domestic market, while maintaining a reasonable balance of distribution between U.S. and foreign carriers.

The six design proposals from the engine and airframe companies were evaluated during the spring of 1964 by government aviation experts and airlines working together. The 210-man government evaluation team under the chairmanship of Deputy Administrator Bain, was drawn from four civilian agencies, FAA, NASA, Civil Aeronautics Board, and the Department of Commerce, and the departments of the Air Force and Navy. The team analyzed more than 130 factors and associated subfactors. An independent evaluation of the proposals was undertaken by an airliner group (American, Braniff, Continental, Delta, Eastern, National, Northwest, Pan American, TWA, and United). In March, 1964, FAA and the ten airlines reviewed both government and airline evaluation findings, and on April 1, the deputy administrator for supersonic transport development forwarded his findings and recommendations to the FAA administrator.

On the same day, President Johnson issued an executive order, creating a new Advisory Committee on Supersonic Transport, consisting of the secretaries of Defense, Treasury, and Commerce, and the administrators of NASA and FAA, as well as "such other members as the President may from time to time appoint." The committee was to study, advise, and make recommendations to the President with regard to all aspects of the SST program, giving special attention to the financial aspects. In June, the FAA awarded six-month airframe contracts to the Boeing Company and the Lockheed Aircraft Corporation, and six-month engine contracts to the Pratt & Whitney Aircraft Division of the United Aircraft Corporation and to the General Electric Company. Each of the airframe contracts totaled $6 million, with the government providing $4.5 million, the remainder of the cost to be borne by the company. Each engine contract totaled $5 million, of which the government provided $3.5 million. Boeing and Lockheed contracted to perform extensive design and structural studies as well as wind tunnel tests aimed at improving and refining their basic proposals to meet technical and economic objectives. The contracts required that wind tunnel models of the refined configurations be available by November 1, 1964, for independent aerodynamic analysis by government laboratories.

General Electric and Pratt & Whitney were asked to develop detailed preliminary layout designs showing that they could meet standards set down for performance, operational reliability, safety, maintainability, and economy.

Sonic Boom and Other Problems

At the same time that the President ordered the SST airframe and engine programs to be carried forward, he directed that sonic boom tests be made under the guidance of the National Academy of Sciences. The FAA had already begun an intensive study of public reactions to sonic booms as they might be produced by supersonic transports. Aircraft were provided for the tests by the Air Force, and NASA provided research guidance and over-all support. The tests began in February, 1964, and continued for twenty-six weeks. During that time, Air Force jets flew 1,253 carefully defined boom runs over Oklahoma City, eight times a day for seven days a week during daylight hours. At the start of the study, the boom overpressure level was 1 pound per square foot. This was raised after a period of time to 1.5 pounds, and at the end of the study it had increased to 2 pounds. A comprehensive report of the findings was published in the spring of 1965.

A study of the effects of sonic booms at higher pressure levels on typical houses and other structures was conducted between November, 1964, and February, 1965, at the White Sands Missile Range, New Mexico. Subjected to 1,494 booms of varying magnitudes during this period were sixteen frame structures, seven of which contained instruments to measure reaction to the booms. Some were residential in type and were furnished. Included were a farmhouse, plate glass store fronts, and a greenhouse. Sonic boom overpressures generated by the Air Force jets ranged from 2 to more than 20 pounds per square foot. The 20-pound level, it was found, could cause detectable structural damage.

Sonic boom problems had not been completely solved by mid-1966, but there were reasons for optimism, and plans for a new series of tests were completed. The locations of the new tests were a closely guarded secret, but did not include Oklahoma City. Tests were expected to be held during the summer and fall of 1967, with Air Force B-58's creating the booms. The communities to be used as guinea pigs were to be given advance warning, but the specific time of each boom would not be made known in advance. A number of night booms would be included.

While design activity and sonic boom study were under way, a flight program being conducted in conjunction with the Air Force at Wright-Patterson Air Force Base, Ohio, and Randolph Air Force Base, Texas, entered a new phase, and FAA's air traffic simulation laboratory at the National Aviation Facilities Experimental Center (NAFEC) at Atlantic City, New Jersey, continued its study of SST problems in air traffic control begun in May, 1963. When an SST flight simulator went into operation at NASA's Langley Research Center, Hampton, Virginia, tie-in was established between it and the NAFEC facilities, so that runs could be conducted in which the four-man simulator crew at Langley "flew" under various test conditions as if actually operating a supersonic transport, while FAA personnel at NAFEC "controlled" the plane as if it were an actual transport in the airways system.

Because the supersonic transport will fly high as well as fast, the Air Force, FAA, and the National Aeronautics and Space Administration designed a series of radiation analysis experiments for the Air Force to run at SST altitudes to determine significant biological effects from natural radiation and to better define the environment to be encountered by supersonic travelers. The radiation-measuring instruments were to be containerized in four packages, distributed among four Air Force aircraft flown at altitudes ranging from 40,000 to 80,000 feet over a wide range of latitudes. Dose rates were to be measured, and types of radiation identified. First flights were planned to start in July, 1966; flights would continue over the next two years, during which time solar activity was expected to reach a maximum. The planes to be used in the tests were RB-57F's, which provide a radiation profile very close to that of the proposed supersonic transport.

DECISIONS AND EVALUATIONS

Reporting on an evaluation of design work pointed toward meeting SST requirements, the FAA administrator told the House Committee on Science and Astronautics in January, 1965: "The second evaluation strongly indicated that there are no significant technical problems that cannot be overcome in an orderly development program, in either airframe or engine development." Major design improvements had been achieved in terms of increased aerodynamic and propulsive efficiency, improved economic characteristics, and higher payload capability.

In March, 1965, the President's Advisory Committee on Supersonic Transport reviewed all major SST programs and concluded that, with future work on basic technological problems successfully concluded, a commercially profitable SST could be developed. The committee also told the President that as much work as possible should be done before beginning construction on the prototype aircraft so that a large part of the financial risk would be minimized. After receiving the committee's recommendations, the President

announced on July 1, 1965, that he had decided the SST program should move into an eighteen-month phase of accelerated design work aimed at starting prototype construction
by the end of 1966. To initiate this stage of the supersonic
development program, the President asked Congress for an
appropriation of $140 million, a threefold increase in the
level of funds then being spent. Late in March, 1966, the newly
appointed FAA Supersonic Transport Program Manager,
Major General Jewell C. Maxwell reported that at least 3,400
hours of flight time would be needed before the FAA could
certificate a supersonic transport, more than twice the usual
certification flight time. The extensive flight test program would
be necessary, General Maxwell warned, because there were
really no advanced military models of the SST. Experience
with the B-70, F-12, and F-111 would be helpful, but operating differences were too great to place complete confidence in
military test data. The FAA supersonic schedule at that time
called for flight-testing one or more prototypes beginning early
in the 1970's, probably over the Air Force's B-70 test range,
which covers a large portion of the western part of the United
States as well as a Pacific Coast corridor about 1,000 miles
long. Many aspects of the SST would have to be investigated
during these prototype test runs. The agency would require that
the automatic or self-checking systems be thoroughly perfected.
Cooling-off periods after landing should be minimal, and not
interfere with normal servicing operations. General Maxwell
pointed out that expansion due to inflight heating would cause
the aircraft to increase one foot in length during each supersonic flight.

Meantime, Captain George T. Henderson, a United Air
Lines official, told a meeting of the Society of Automotive
Engineers: "I only wish our economy could, and would support the development of two competitive SST's all the way
through, so that each operator would have the final selection
as to the equipment he would be laying out such tremendous

sums of money to purchase." On the day when Captain Henderson spoke, his company still had been unable to make up its mind about the kind of SST it wanted. Although it had sent design teams to Europe to study the Anglo-French Concorde and had also participated in every one of the U.S. design evaluation studies, United had delayed placing purchase orders for either SST. Later, United placed orders for both planes.

In April, 1966, Eastern Airlines submitted an advance payment of $200,000 to FAA to reserve two delivery positions for a supersonic transport. The Eastern transaction raised the total number of reserve delivery positions to ninety-six, and the total number of companies holding reservations to twenty-two. Each of the ninety-six reserve delivery positions was backed by an advance royalty payment of $100,000. This money—a total of $9.6 million—was kept as an interest-free deposit in the U.S. Treasury. Earlier in 1966, Panagra, which was then changing ownership, canceled its two SST reservations, and the government refunded the airline's $200,000 in advance royalty payments. By early 1967, FAA had in hand 26 orders for 113 aircraft.

Final evaluation of SST prototype proposals was done by a team of government experts working in great secrecy. Administrator McKee emphasized that the airlines were brought into every phase of the program. Every step of the way to SST selection was taken "hand in hand" with the ultimate users of the aircraft. After a 1966 White House press briefing, McKee told reporters that the plan was to build two copies of a single prototype design. To fund two different SST models and carry them through prototype flight stages would simply be putting off the final decision. Furthermore, almost exactly twice as much money would be needed to build one prototype of each of the two designs as to build two copies of the same design, and by putting off the decision until both types of planes were flying, the program could be delayed another year or more. Two copies of the same design must be built, McKee insisted, then in case something happened to one, there would always be the second prototype to continue the research, development, and design refinement work.

Assuming a solution to the sonic boom and other problems, the flight of the first prototype aircraft was expected in 1970, and the first deliveries would be made to the user airlines in 1974.

THE WINNERS

Exactly on schedule, FAA Administrator McKee, on December 31, 1966, announced the winners of the supersonic transport design competition. The Boeing Company was the winner for the airframe and the General Electric Company for the engine. The selection ended the intensive thirty-month competition between Boeing and Lockheed and between General Electric and Pratt & Whitney. In his New Year's Eve announcement, General McKee said that the choice of Boeing and General Electric "is supported by a comprehensive government evaluation and by the majority of the major U.S. airlines as well as independent technical analyses."

The announcement was received by the airline industry and the public with considerable interest, but with a surprising lack of critical comment. Even those congressmen who in the past had been quick to criticize the Administration's decisions to buy military aircraft were silent when General McKee announced his choice of builders of the U.S. supersonic plane. While public comment was at a minimum, private discussions by agency officials were not. It was pointed out that the Boeing swing-wing design had a lower landing speed, and required less power for take-off. This meant that the operating noise level near airports would be lower than that for the Lockheed design. This fact alone would have put Boeing out in front in the design competition. The Boeing SST also had better sonic boom characteristics. Another deciding factor was the selection of the Boeing design by a majority of the U.S. airlines participating in the evaluation. Foreign flag airlines, for the most part, declined to name a choice. It was said that price was not an important element in the choice of the airframe, although it may have played some part in the engine selection, since the simple General Electric engine design made a price saving almost certain.

On April 29, 1967, four months after the winners of the competition had been announced, President Johnson authorized the Secretary of Transportation to sign the contracts that would bring the first U.S. supersonic transports into being. Eighty per cent of the cost of the first three years' work would be borne by the government, and 20 per cent by the companies building the airframes and the engines and by the airlines that had ordered the transports. The government's share in this largest U.S. aviation project ever undertaken would be paid back into the treasury as the giant transports were sold.

Whether the FAA will continue to manage the supersonic transport construction program is, at this writing, unclear. Secretary of Transportation Alan Boyd is known to favor the establishment of a special government corporation, similar to the Communications Satellite Corporation, to take over responsibility for the SST. To make this change, both President Johnson and Congress will first have to be persuaded that it is necessary, and if Secretary Boyd has reason to believe that strong objections may be raised, management of the SST program may very well be retained by the FAA, at least during Boyd's tenure in office.

XIV

FAA and the Future

The future of the Federal Aviation Administration is now tied directly to the future of the Department of Transportation. Will hoped-for improvements in the administration of FAA and in its research and development effort materialize, now that it is a branch of the newest of the departments? Or will the fears of those who opposed the transfer of FAA to the Department of Transportation be realized?

This opposition, for the most part, came from private and business aviation interests. The scheduled airlines, at congressional hearings early in 1966, took a position which was neither completely favorable nor clearly in opposition to the Administration's efforts to establish a department of transportation. Both the FAA administrator and the chairman of the Civil Aeronautics Board supported the Administration proposal at the hearings, as did the Under Secretary of Commerce. The Bureau of the Budget, not unexpectedly, went on record strongly favoring the plan.

The National Business Aircraft Association took about as strong a position against the change as any group. The association's executive director, William K. Lawton, said that the bills proposed would (1) give major transportation policy consideration only to common carriers, (2) vest the government agency controlling the entire aviation regulatory, procedural, and operational complex with authority to investi-

211

gate aviation accidents for which the agency itself may have been responsible, (3) do away with the present independent appeal processes on revocations or suspensions of airmen, aircraft, or other air certificates, and (4) submerge the present independent FAA into a department of transportation overseeing and controlling highway, rail, water, barge-line, aviation, Coast Guard, and pipeline activities. Policies for all modes would be established without any control over routes or rates, according to the present bills, Mr. Lawton said, emphasizing the word "present." The principal reason given for establishment of the new department was a need for "coordination," but the existing job description of the Under Secretary of Commerce for Transportation already provided for this coordination task. Mr. Lawton urged that appropriate congressional and executive action be taken to assist the under secretary in fulfilling this assignment.

Flying magazine in its June, 1966, issue spoke up for private flyers and those who fly for pleasure. "With encouragement, all of aviation will flourish. Buried in a department and headed by a cabinet member beseiged by the pressures and woes of the railroads, the interstate buses, the newly recognized hazards of the automobile and a second-rate maritime fleet, who knows how aviation would fare," wrote Robert Parke, editor of *Flying*. "It looks to us as if all of aviation can grow if its present state with a separate agency and a full-time deputy administrator for general aviation affairs is maintained."

Perhaps the most telling argument against submerging the FAA in another Cabinet agency was made by former CAA Administrator Frederick B. Lee, who pointed out that aviation is an unusual form of transport because it is so comparatively new. Ground and water transportation are using equipment that has long been highly developed, and the problems of these modes are largely concerned with efficient administration, safety, and labor relations. In 1955, when the

CAA was a subordinate branch of the Commerce Department, Administrator Lee's biggest problem was getting sufficient funds for the air safety needs of the growing aviation community.

The most articulate spokesman in favor of changing the FAA's independent status was Alan S. Boyd. In 1965, Boyd had left the Civil Aeronautics Board, where almost everyone agreed he had been doing an outstanding job, to become Under Secretary of Commerce for Transportation, with the task of selling the idea of a new department of transportation to Congress and the affected industries. As part of his campaign, Boyd gave an interview to *Aviation Daily,* published March 11, 1966, predicting early congressional approval of the President's proposal for a new department. Congressional sentiment was eight to one in favor of the Administration's plan, according to Mr. Boyd, who also said he expected minimum opposition from the various affected industries. In this respect, the *Aviation Daily* said, Under Secretary Boyd's analysis might be at least partly correct, since the Air Transport Association was reportedly going to take either a neutral position or one conditionally favoring the new department. In the interview, Boyd sought to quiet fears that the department ultimately would also absorb two independent transport regulatory agencies—the Civil Aeronautics Board and the Interstate Commerce Commission—as well as the Maritime Administration of the Department of Commerce. Boyd said such a move would be "inconceivable." Boyd wholeheartedly advocated the President's proposal for a national safety board, which would be located, for administrative purposes, in the new department, but would be headed by five Presidential appointees. He did not share the concern of those in aviation who questioned that part of the President's plan that would take away from CAB its accident investigation authority. CAB members usually devoted only about 10 per cent of their time to safety matters, claimed

Boyd, whereas the proposed national board, although it would be concerned with the safety of other modes of transportation, would nevertheless work full time on safety questions, resulting in a more intensified effort on safety for all transport modes, including aviation.

CAB Chairman Charles S. Murphy, late in March, 1966, also endorsed the idea of a department of transportation. He told a luncheon meeting of the Los Angeles Chamber of Commerce that "support for the President's recommendation appears to be widespread and substantial," but that the board "will be saddened" by the departure of its safety staff, because "the Board has taken a special pride in the performance of its safety functions." He endorsed the idea of allowing a secretary of transportation to set criteria for subsidy awards to the local service carriers. Specific determination of subsidy payments would continue to remain with the CAB under the President's proposal. This was as it should be, the CAB chairman explained, since CAB is in the best position to perform subsidy allocation functions because of its jurisdiction over routes, operating authority, and fares. "If anyone can eliminate the need for subsidy," said Murphy, "it is the CAB and it should have the job."

On April 7, 1966, FAA Administrator McKee testified before the House Government Operations Subcommittee, which was holding hearings on the Administration's bill H.R. 13200, setting up the new agency: "The department will provide for a better level of ability to match total intercity transportation capacity to demand. Overexpansion and imbalance between modes will be avoided." McKee admitted that total federal funding for transportation work was likely to increase, but that it would probably increase less under the coordinated direction of a secretary of transportation. The supersonic transport program would continue in the new department very much as it would in an independent FAA, and it would be possible for the secretary to veto future supersonic funds, just as the Secretary of Defense has from time to time declined to use money that Congress appropriated for the purchase of manned bombers.

Early in April, 1966, Senator A. S. Mike Monroney, of Oklahoma, the "father" of the Federal Aviation Act and chairman of the Senate Aviation Subcommittee, wrote to Senator John L. McClellan of Arkansas, chairman of the Senate Government Operations Committee, that he was concerned lest the transfer of FAA "result in a return to neglect and indifference toward air safety and promotion of aviation." Senator Monroney also questioned the wisdom of transferring accident investigation responsibilities from the CAB to the new department. He pointed out that aviation accident investigation required skills largely unrelated to railroad, automobile, or maritime accidents, and advised Senator McClellan that he would propose several perfecting amendments to the bill setting up the new agency.

The idea of a department of transportation is not a new one. The Bureau of the Budget was making plans for a department of transportation when two midair collisions in the spring of 1958 made it impossible to hold Congress back any longer in its drive to set up the independent Federal Aviation Agency. But the idea of a department of transportation did not originate with the Budget Bureau. As long ago as March, 1949, when the Hoover Commission submitted its recommendations to Congress on the reorganization of the Commerce Department, the commission unanimously disagreed with a task force suggestion that a department of transportation be created. Instead, the commission recommended grouping within the Department of Commerce all the major nonregulatory transportation activities of the federal government, replacing the CAA with a bureau of civil aviation authorized to issue and enforce all air safety rules. The Civil Aeronautics Board would exercise only a review function responsibility for such air safety rules. It was also recommended that aeronautical research being done by the National Advisory Committee for Aeronautics be brought under the proposed Bureau of Civil Aviation.

In May, 1950, President Truman's Reorganization Plan Number Five, based in part on the recommendations of the Hoover Commission, transferred to the Secretary of Commerce all functions of all government aviation agencies and officials, except those of the CAB. The organization plan led to the creation of an Office of Transportation within the Department of Commerce, headed by an under secretary. This had the effect of placing a layer of supervision between the CAA administrator and the Secretary of Commerce, and this, in turn, made for problems that eventually had to be solved through the creation of the independent Federal Aviation Agency. At the present writing, some feel that the cycle may be starting all over again. In Washington, sometimes it seems that Hegel was right: "People and governments have never learned anything from history or acted on principles deduced from it." The transportation act was passed; the FAA is again a subordinate agency in a Cabinet-level department.

PLANNING FOR THE FUTURE

If the past is imperfectly understood, or the future too dimly seen, it is not for want of trying. Under both Administrators Quesada and Halaby, the FAA tried to study the past problems of aviation and to relate these to possible future problems and future solutions. This kind of forward planning is continuing under Administrator McKee, but at a reduced level and with more emphasis on specific future problems. For example, to meet "black-out" problems caused by inadequate long-range air-to-ground and air-to-air communications over the North Atlantic, FAA, early in 1966, began evaluation of a Communications Satellite Corporation proposal, which would help solve communication black-out problems at a cost estimated at less than $10 million. The proposed solution was a two-channel satellite with a usable life of four to five years. Hughes Aircraft Company would be contractor for the satellite, which would weigh about 210 pounds and be placed precisely in a synchronous equatorial orbit—the equivalent of a fixed position over the North Atlantic, from which the satellite could relay communications from aircraft anywhere on the North Atlantic both to other aircraft and to ground stations on either side of the ocean.

Aircraft population forecasts are prepared annually by FAA, as part of planning for the future. Latest forecast is that the U.S. domestic scheduled airlines will carry nearly 160 million passengers and fly almost 113 billion revenue passenger miles by the end of 1970, almost twice the mileage flown during 1965, when U.S. air carriers carried 95 million passengers 63 billion revenue passenger miles.

In addition to scheduled airline traffic increases, FAA's planning staff anticipate that the total airline fleet will increase from its 1965 level of about 2,100 planes to about 2,400 at the end of the five-year planning period. Jet aircraft are expected to triple in number from 564 planes to 1,690 aircraft. Among the jets, two- and three-engine types will increase from an inventory of 108 to nearly 1,000.

One area of particularly rapid expected growth is the air taxi business. FAA recognized this potential growth in 1965 when it took steps to increase the equipment and operational standards of the 3,300 air taxi operators and commercial operators of small aircraft. In its annual report for 1965, FAA told Congress:

> Need for the new standard was underscored by the recent marked increase in the complexity and volume of air taxi operations. The scheduled air taxi is becoming a popular means of transportation where small airports are located near industry or population centers, or where trunkline and local service carrier

scheduling does not meet business travel needs. Manufacturers are designing small aircraft suited to the requirements of the air taxi operators. Route carriers have recently recognized the potential of air taxi operators to serve as traffic feeders and are entering into operating agreements with them. This trend of rapidly increasing air taxi operations during the next few years also means an increase in FAA surveillance and inspection.

One of FAA's most ambitious efforts to look into the future took place in 1961, when President Kennedy directed FAA Administrator Halaby to develop a statement of the technical, economic, and military goals of commercial and military aviation for the 1961–70 period. The goals were to be definite enough to make possible practical long-range planning. This study, called Project Horizon, was undertaken by an eight-man task force of aviation experts. Chairman was Fred M. Glass, business executive and a member of the 1955 Harding Aviation Facilities Study Group.

In September, 1961, the White House released the Project Horizon report. President Kennedy endorsed the task force's recommendations, instructed the FAA administrator to put them into effect, and instructed the Secretary of Commerce to take the proposal into account in preparing a report on overall national transportation policies.

The 239-page Project Horizon report defined twenty-four national aviation goals, and outlined the various action programs which were needed to achieve these goals. Among the major goals were: (1) maintenance of U.S. leadership in world aviation; (2) a basic change in the government's approach to the economic regulation of the airlines to avoid a threatened collapse in the financial condition of the carriers; (3) development of a 2,000-mile-an-hour supersonic transport aircraft; (4) renewed emphasis on aeronautical, as opposed to astronautical, aspects of government research and development; (5) a detailed study of international aviation affairs, to be commissioned by the President; (6) enactment of legislation, tailored to aviation's needs, to replace the Railway Labor Act; (7) continued effort to achieve a common civil-military air traffic control and air navigation system; and (8) establishment, within the FAA, of a Federal Aviation Agency Service, which could become an integral part of the military services in time of war.

Often FAA's projections err on the conservative side. FAA planners, for example, have consistently underestimated the growth rate of general aviation, which at times has expanded at twice the rate forecast by FAA. In January, 1967, the Aerospace Industries Association reported that 1,161 light aircraft were shipped by U.S. manufacturers. During the preceding six months, U.S. light-plane builders had shipped more general aviation planes than the total number of planes operated by all the airlines in the Free World. Terminal facilities to handle general aviation have not kept pace. The Aerospace Industries Association reported that, unless additional airports are created in Los Angeles, by 1970 it will not be feasible for an individual or a business to purchase an airplane, because there will be no place to base it in the immediate area.

Some experts maintain that helicopters are the answer to both airport and city congestion problems. Helicopters, however, have many problems of their own. One of these is all-weather operation. It was not until March, 1965, that the FAA certificated the first helicopter carrier to conduct instrument operations. The carrier, Los Angeles Airways, was limited in the initial FAA approval to instrument flight departures from, and approaches to, Los Angeles International Airport. The remainder of each flight had to be conducted under visual flight rules. As Los Angeles Airways gained experience with instrument flight rule operations, the extent to which its flights might be conducted under instrument rules would be increased; eventually, it was hoped, the helicopter operator could be certificated for instrument operations over its entire system.

In October, 1964, twelve Los Angeles Airways pilots became the first helicopter pilots authorized by FAA to seek qualifications for conducting air carrier helicopter operations under instrument flight rules. The authorization was made under interim standards, pending formal codification of standards for this rating into the Federal Air Regulations.

Another helicopter air carrier, New York Airways, was expected during fiscal 1966 to be certificated for instrument flight operations. New York Airways in 1965 already had approved equipment for such operations, and qualification of pilots was under way.

To dramatize the important way in which helicopters can be utilized for city-center to city-center transportation, Administrator McKee made use of "choppers" at both ends of a Washington to New York trip to make a speech in midtown Manhattan early in 1966. In his talk, he described his trip from Washington to New York:

> Just a little more than an hour ago I was at my desk at my office in Washington. It was time to go. I climbed the one flight of stairs to our rooftop heliport, boarded a helicopter and zipped across the Potomac to Washington National Airport. I flew by jet to Kennedy where another chopper waited. Flying time from Kennedy to the new Pan Am Heliport was seven minutes. It may be that I now hold the speed record from downtown Washington to downtown New York.

Administrator McKee's "pad-to-pad" travel time was exactly sixty-three minutes. The trip also served as a dramatic demonstration of the worth of the Pan Am helicopter landing pad on the roof of the Pan Am Building in midtown Manhattan. Commercial service from Pan Am's helipad began December 21, 1965, with a schedule of seventeen incoming and eighteen outgoing flights per day. Fare was $7.00 for a one-way, seven-minute trip from Kennedy Airport.

Despite General McKee's endorsement of the helicopter

as the quickest city-center to airport method of travel, there were objections to the midtown helipad in New York by local residents, who were disturbed by noise as well as by the risk inherent in low-flying over the city. The volume of complaints reached such a point in March, 1966, that the New York City Department of Marine and Aviation said it would take another look at the situation to see if the Pan Am heliport should be allowed to remain in operation or should be closed as a hazard. This was the first study of the facility since it began operations on December 21, 1965, on top of the fifty-nine-story building adjacent to Grand Central Terminal. Department of Marine and Aviation licenses are issued on a year-to-year basis and can be revoked at any time. The New York City Commissioner, however, said that Pan Am's $800,000 heliport installation would not be closed without careful consultation with the Mayor and the City Planning Commission. The heliport had been approved in 1965 only after extensive studies by the Planning Commission and five years of additional study and approval by both federal and local agencies.

The other two New York City commercial heliports require flight plans that avoid passing over Manhattan at all. The West Thirtieth Street heliport is used only when poor visibility makes taking off or landing at the Pan Am Building impossible. The Wall Street heliport in early 1966 served thirty daily flights to and from Kennedy Airport, twenty-eight Newark flights, and twenty-three between the heliport and La Guardia Airport. Traffic from the Wall Street heliport flew over Manhattan until October, 1965, when protests by civic groups forced a rerouting over the East River.

IN TIME OF WAR

FAA's planning for the future includes a number of studies of what the agency's role should be if the United

States should become involved in a major war—particularly a war which involved an attack on the population centers of the United States. During fiscal 1965, the FAA began preparing a defense readiness plan for its headquarters. As part of this plan, the FAA Washington headquarters building was surveyed and approved for use as a public shelter. By the end of fiscal 1965, the shelter was stocked with supplies sufficient to sustain 4,000 people for two weeks. In addition, a shelter management plan was developed, together with the necessary staff assignments. Civil defense exercises were conducted to test the headquarters' emergency organizational concepts and procedures. One of the principal findings of this test was that the agency's emergency relocation site was inadequate, and a comprehensive study was ordered to find a more suitable site. A cryptographic teletypewriter system was installed, linking FAA headquarters, regional headquarters, and the air route traffic control centers. The system was flexible enough to permit transmission of classified information between the FAA and the military services. Arrangements also were made during fiscal 1965 to obtain off-line cryptographic devices from the Department of Defense that would enable the FAA, in case of attack, to send classified information over any surviving teletypewriter circuit. The agency took measures to protect its air route traffic control centers from sabotage or other unlawful acts. Guards were provided for all centers, fences, security lighting, control buildings, and other safety features were installed. The FAA also compiled a "safe-haven airport" list, comprising about 500 airports having acceptable probability of survival as well as suitability for air carrier operations in case of a nuclear attack.

In 1964, the President directed the FAA and the Department of Defense to plan for the likelihood that, in time of war, FAA would become an adjunct to the Department of Defense. Under this concept, FAA would remain organizationally intact, but the administrator's responsibility for FAA statutory functions would be subject to the authority, direction, and control of the Secretary of Defense to the extent deemed necessary by the Secretary, including the placing of FAA operational elements under the direct control of military commanders.

Because of its air traffic control responsibilities for the military, the FAA became directly involved in the Cuban missile crisis, as noted in Chapter XI. What is not so generally known is that FAA controllers are also active in the Viet-Nam conflict. Because of the defense build-up, the Tan Son Nhut Airport at Saigon by 1966 had become the busiest in the world. Air traffic volume early in 1966 exceeded that at Chicago's O'Hare Field, which, until then, had been the world's busiest airport. In addition to commercial passenger and cargo flights, the Saigon Airport handles a large number of military operations. One of the ironies of the war in Southeast Asia is that a tourist, as of this writing, can buy a regular ticket on a commercial flight and land in the middle of the war. Because of the very real danger, FAA personnel are chosen from a number of volunteers for two-year Saigon assignments.

In his last report to President Eisenhower, former FAA Administrator Quesada took a perceptive look ahead:

> Aviation is at a crucial crossroad. Its continued healthy growth will require a higher order of leadership and vigorous, imaginative effort on the part of the government, cooperation of the aviation industry, and the understanding support of the American public. It will also require on the part of special interest groups, wider acceptance of the principle that the advocacy of parochial points of view cannot be allowed to subvert the public interest. For over thirty years now, as a pilot, as a friend of aviation, as a government official, I have had the privilege of working for progress in air transportation. I am confident that with the common will to succeed, aviation can continue to

forge ahead in the years to come and successfully meet the challenges with which it is now confronted.

When FAA Administrator Halaby left office, he recounted some of the accomplishments of the agency under his administration. For FAA and civil aviation alike, he said, "the greatest challenge will continue to be the wise management for the safe and efficient use of the airspace. . . . As advances in technology will surely increase the speed and economic feasibility of carrying people and goods by air over both the short interurban and long intercontinental stage lengths, we must only be sure that government policies and programs do not inhibit the potentiality from becoming the reality."

Appendix A

The Lost Pilot: Transcript of a Tape Recording

There is a fraternity of the air that flourishes in flying clubs, over coffee cups, and in hangar sessions at a thousand airports across the country. The fraternal feeling of this group is never more clearly demonstrated than when a felow pilot is lost. The following account is the transcript of an actual taped radio transmission, slightly condensed, telling the story of such a pilot, lost in the fog and cloud layers above California in the wintertime, while en route from Riverside to Redding with two passengers. It is also the story of an FAA air traffic controller, of an airline pilot, and of another light plane pilot, all of whom join forces in an attempt to bring the lost pilot and his aircraft safely to earth.

This transcript, which originally appeared in *FAA Aviation News* of March, 1963, is presented here to dramatize the hazards faced by an inexperienced pilot who failed to make the 180-degree turn that might have got him back out of the weather before it was too late. The lost pilot and his aircraft are identified throughout by the fictitious call sign *Nan XYZ*. The other major characters in this drama can be identified as: George Baldwin, air traffic controller at FAA's Oakland Air Route Traffic Control Center and an experienced pilot himself, familiar with the XYZ type; Captain Milo Kopp, in command of United Air Lines Flight No. 388; and Louis Pelletier, pilot of the Piper Aztec N4875P.

RED BLUFF FLIGHT SERVICE STATION: Oakland Center, this is Red Bluff radio. We have a little problem with an aircraft—Nan XYZ—not sure of his position. We can give him steers into Red Bluff. We want to know if you have any traffic.

225

OAKLAND AIR ROUTE TRAFFIC CONTROL CENTER: I have traffic at four thousand. Is he VFR?

RED BLUFF: Oh no. He's in the soup at two thousand.

OAKLAND: ATC requests XYZ contact the Oakland Center one one eight point four or one two five point seven now for radar identification and steers into Red Bluff.

NAN XYZ: This is XYZ. Where in the hell am I now?

OAKLAND: XYZ, climb and maintain four thousand, over.

XYZ: This is XYZ. I read you, and I am climbing out.

OAKLAND: Do you have VOR equipment?

XYZ: I don't know what I've got.

OAKLAND: Roger. XYZ, remain on this frequency. How much more fuel do you have? Over.

XYZ: About one-quarter of a tank—about three-quarters of an hour. I don't know where in hell I'm at.

OAKLAND: Roger, XYZ. What is your present heading?

XYZ: I am flying at twenty-nine degrees.

UNITED AIR LINES FLIGHT NO. 388: XYZ, this is United Air Lines. What is your estimated position? Over.

XYZ: I have no idea.

UNITED: Where did you take off from and how long have you been flying on what heading?

XYZ: I took off at Riverside. I have been flying for three hours and forty-five minutes.

OAKLAND: Roger. What is your present heading? Over.

XYZ: My present heading? I am going pretty near due east—due west three degrees.

OAKLAND: Roger, XYZ. We're trying to get a fix on you now. Over.

XYZ: I am heading due north.

OAKLAND: Roger, XYZ. Make right triangular turns two minutes. Over.

XYZ: Got yah.

OAKLAND: Roger. Amend that to one minute leg. On your right turn, fly one minute. Make a right turn, fly one minute on that leg and continue, and we will see if we can pick you up. Go ahead.

XYZ: I still have no idea where I'm at.

OAKLAND: XYZ, can you give me your compass heading now—your compass heading?

XYZ: North twenty-four degrees [unintelligible] dead west right now.

OAKLAND: Is that two four zero—two four zero degrees?

XYZ: I don't understand what you want. Get me out of this fog up here. Get me to hell out of here.

OAKLAND: Roger, XYZ. Your compass heading, can you give me your compass heading? You're flying by compass, you have a compass in front of you there now—if you'll just take a look at that and give me the reading off it.

XYZ: We are flying due west.

OAKLAND: Roger. That's a two seven zero heading—compass heading.

XYZ: I believe that's what it is. It's a fog. We're still in a fog at seven thousand feet. We're still in the fog flying due west twenty degrees. I have no idea of what I am even doing.

UNITED: XYZ, do you read United?

XYZ: I read you but I have no idea what I'm doing.

OAKLAND: XYZ. We believe we have you in radar contact now, approximately forty-five miles south, southwest of Red Bluff. Can you take up a heading of zero eight five for about two minutes? Over.

XYZ: Zero eight five. I have no idea of what the hell it is. I'll tell you the truth about it.

OAKLAND: Okay be sure and keep your airspeed up. Keep your airspeed up above hundred. Continue your climb on up to about ten thousand. Over.

XYZ: Got yah.

UNITED: Center, United three eighty-eight. I believe if he just takes a cardinal heading like east, it probably will be a little easier for him to understand at this time. Just relax a little bit.

OAKLAND: Okay, fine. Thanks, United.

OAKLAND: XYZ, take zero eight five heading—only five degrees off of east. Just take up east on your compass, east. Over.

UNITED: United. Do you read now?

XYZ: I read you, but I don't know what I'm doing.

UNITED: Okay now, just relax. We all get in a spot once in a while. If you'll just relax your hands on the wheel, just for a second,

I think we'll calm down. Take your feet off the rudders for a second, and then just shake your hands a bit and relax and go back to it and just head east which is "E" on the indicator. East heading, and hold that for a minute or so. Just nice and straight and I think we can calm down quite a bit and accomplish quite a bit. Okay?

XYZ: Okay, I got yah.

UNITED: You have a good airplane under you. It's a real good machine, and with just a little help, it will do a real good job for you.

XYZ: We are going due east now at nine thousand feet.

UNITED: Very good, very good, fine. Just hold that now, and you'll be doing real good.

XYZ: My gas is getting down below a quarter of a tank.

UNITED: We all make mistakes. Relax, and now we'll get out of this real good.

OAKLAND: United, this is Oakland. He should have a reserve—after he goes on empty—he should have five or six gallons. We show him now about forty-five miles, bearing approximately two zero zero from Red Bluff.

UNITED 388: Roger. If you could work him down in the Sacramento Valley, there's lots of airports in the Sacramento Valley which he can distinguish very easily.

OAKLAND: XYZ, continue your present heading. It will take about another twenty miles to get you over into the valley. Over.

UNITED: XYZ, from United. Your position is probably west of the Sacramento Valley, up near Red Bluff, and the Center is going to take you east over to the valley, and then drop you down in the valley, where you'll have a lot better weather.

XYZ: Okay. I got it. We will hold an east heading and keep on climbing out.

UNITED: That's right, you keep that east heading now, and we'll tell you when you're ready to descend and that'll put you in the valley. So you listen to him and relax a little more. I think once in a while, just take your hands off the wheel and shake them a little bit and go back, and it'll be pretty easy for you. I would set up a cruise now with your mixture leaned out so you can conserve your fuel.

OAKLAND: XYZ, what altitude you at now? Over.

XYZ: We're up at ninety-five hundred feet, and we're having trouble.

OAKLAND: Roger. And what is your present heading? Are you still heading east? Over.

XYZ: We are heading now east—we're heading north.

UNITED: XYZ, from United. Now if we trim the airplane back into a right turn, back to an easterly heading, and stop on the easterly heading, hold it there. We'll be getting over the valley.

OAKLAND: Take up a heading of one eight zero, which is south on your compass, south on your compass. Maintain that heading until further advised. Be sure and keep up your airspeed, and, as United said, relax on your controls. Over.

UNITED: Okay, if you'll right rudder into a right turn to a southerly heading. Head south—"S" on the compass, and hold that. The center is working you very well now.

XYZ: You want me to go which direction?

UNITED: Want you to go south, south. Relax, we're working on you, so just relax if you can. I know it's hard, but we can do it.

XYZ: This is XYZ. We're having trouble.

OAKLAND: XYZ, this is Oakland Center. You appear to be over low terrain at the present time—over low terrain. If you'll just take up a southerly heading, head south, head south. Make a real gradual turn.

UNITED: XYZ from United. Just turn to a south heading now, just turn nice and easy to the south heading, and hold it south. Okay?

OAKLAND: XYZ, settle down now, settle down now. Head south, south on your compass. Be sure and keep your airspeed up. Make a gradual descent, a gradual descent to seven thousand. Be sure and keep your airspeed above a hundred knots. Over.

UNITED: XYZ, now if you'll—when you get to your southerly heading—if you'll make your descent to seven thousand, you'll be in good shape.

XYZ: This is XYZ. We're way out of control!

OAKLAND: XYZ, let the controls go. Just let XYZ release the controls. Release the controls. Just let go of them. Over.

XYZ: I got yah.

OAKLAND: XYZ, don't worry about your airspeed picking up.

Just relax. The airplane will come out of it on its own. If you have at least seven thousand feet, you'll be all right in your present position. There's clear weather about twenty-five miles to the south. As soon as the airplane recovers, try to take up a southerly heading. Over.

XYZ: The tank is empty!

OAKLAND: You'll have about five gallons. Five gallons will take you where you have to go. Has the airplane righted itself and can you tell me your airspeed? Over.

XYZ: My airspeed is about one hundred and ten miles an hour.

OAKLAND: If you have one ten you're all right. You are all right. If you were in a spin or in any kind of spiral, it should be in excess of that if your trim is on normal. Was your trim normal when you started, when you went on instruments? Over.

OAKLAND: At a hundred and ten knots you should be all right. Head south, head south, just "S" up there on your compass, your liquid compass.

XYZ: This is XYZ we're at fifty-five hundred feet, and at the present time we are going straight north, thirty-three degrees.

OAKLAND: You are heading now towards higher terrain. Turn right, turn right, back to south, back to south. Make your turn with your rudders. Just use a little right rudder pressure, right rudder pressure, that's all—not very much, just a little—just keep your hands off the wheel. Don't use the wheel, don't pull back on it or push forward, just use a little right rudder.

OAKLAND: Nan four eight seven five papa, Oakland Center. Will you give XYZ a call? He's about twenty-five miles north of your present position, and see if you can raise him?

PIPER AZTEC N4875P: Okay. XYZ, Aztec seven five pop.

XYZ: XYZ. I'm at six thousand feet, heading—This thing won't stay straight!

PIPER: Okay, just steady down. Just try to keep around the "S" and around a hundred and ten miles an hour. If you can descend to about five thousand, you'll break out of this bottom layer. We're at forty-five hundred right now, between layers, and we'll try to keep an eye out for you. We'll turn our landing light on. Oakland, seven five. Do you have us both on radar?

OAKLAND: Four eight seven five pop, affirmative. I have seven five pop. I do not have the XYZ. That last known position of the XYZ was about twelve miles east of Red Bluff. If he heads southerly, he should be all right. Over.

PIPER: Yeah [unintelligible] If you want me to stay where I am, I'm about forty-five hundred and I am VFR, and I'll stay on victor two three and work up towards Red Bluff, and maybe I can see him when he comes out.

OAKLAND: Okay, fine. Do you have a flasher on your airplane? Over.

PIPER: Yeah, we got a rotating beacon, and we'll turn the landing light on too.

OAKLAND: Okay, fine, thanks a lot. The estimated position of the XYZ from your present position is about seventeen miles due north, due north. Over.

XYZ: This is XYZ. I am flying at six thousand feet due south.

OAKLAND: Okay, XYZ. Make a nice gradual descent now to about five thousand feet, five thousand. You should have another aircraft at your twelve o'clock position, that is right off the nose, about fifteen miles. Do not gain excessive airspeed in descent; the best way to do it would be just to roll a very slight amount of trim forward. Just roll the trim forward a little, and let the airplane come down by itself.

XYZ: Will you repeat that again?

OAKLAND: Just drop the nose a little bit. Don't pick up any excess speed. Hold your airspeed just as low as you can, around a hundred and ten, a hundred fifteen. Over.

PIPER: Oakland Center, seven five. I think I've got him. I'm going to flash my light. XYZ, do you see a light ahead of you?

XYZ: Yes I do!

PIPER: That's us! Come on over, and we'll take you to Red Bluff.

OAKLAND: Okay. Take over from here, four eight seven five pop. I think he's got I would say not more than about ten minutes fuel.

PIPER: Okay, I think we can almost see the lights of Red Bluff. If you'll clear me for an approach to Red Bluff I'll go slow enough, and I think he can follow me.

OAKLAND: Nan four eight seven five pop, you are cleared for an approach to the Red Bluff Airport.

PIPER: Okay, I'm cleared for an approach. Now I'll slow down to about a hundred miles an hour. You follow me and we'll go into Red Bluff and get down.

OAKLAND: XYZ, are you in the clear now completely? Over.

XYZ: I believe I am.

OAKLAND: Okay, fine. The lights should be on at Red Bluff shortly. Just follow four eight seven five pop. You don't need to talk to us anymore. Over.

UNITED: Oakland Center from United three eighty-eight. Sorry I couldn't help you any more. We'll change over now to Seattle Center.

OAKLAND: Okay. Fine job. Thanks a lot.

XYZ: I'm at forty-five hundred feet now. Where am I now?

PIPER: You just keep coming toward me and [unintelligible]. We are going right straight to Red Bluff now.

OAKLAND: Nan four eight seven five papa, talk a little more to XYZ, will you please? I believe it helps him.

XYZ: This is XYZ. I am four thousand feet, and I'm following you.

PIPER: Okay, now. There's a light area up—it ought to be off your right wing—where Red Bluff is. Now I'm going to slow down to about ninety, so you'll be able to catch me, I think. My compass right now is reading three zero, on the magnetic compass. We are going northwest.

OAKLAND: Nan four eight seven five papa, how far are you from the Red Bluff Airport now? Over.

PIPER: I'm not absolutely sure of it. I would say probably about twenty miles.

OAKLAND: XYZ, how are you doing now. Do you have the other aircraft in sight yet? Over.

XYZ: I am following him.

OAKLAND: Okay, fine. I just wanted to talk to you to see how you were doing. Don't pay any attention to your fuel. Just follow him as long as you can. If it konks out, why then I'll talk to you further.

PIPER: XYZ, seven five pop. The cloud cover doesn't go all the way to the ground underneath us. We'll have quite a bit to see when we get out underneath too.

OAKLAND: Seven five pop and XYZ, the Red Bluff weather is estimated one thousand eight hundred overcast, visibility three miles with haze. You'll have plenty VFR after you break out.

PIPER: Thank you, Oakland.

XYZ: This is XYZ. Are you descending?

PIPER: No, no. We're about, oh, forty-one hundred feet right now. You can stay right there with us. We'll stay at that altitude until we get up over the airport.

XYZ: I'm at forty-two, and you look like you're lower than I am.

PIPER: Okay, we'll stay at forty-one.

OAKLAND: Nan four eight seven five pop and XYZ, the Red Bluff altimeter—three zero zero six, over.

XYZ: This is XYZ. Are you going up?

PIPER: Just a little bit. We are watching you and we are just about to Red Bluff now. Hang on. Okay, XYZ. We are over the Red Bluff Airport right now—now I'm going to make a real slow turn to the right and you follow me right on around, and we are going to head back down the valley the way we were coming up, and let down.

XYZ: This is XYZ. Are you descending?

PIPER: Not quite yet. I want to wait till you catch up with me now and get in line, because the heading that I'm on right now is the heading we are going to use to let down on.

XYZ: This is XYZ. What are you doing—turning?

PIPER: No, we are going straight ahead. Now our compass reads about one four one four, XYZ. Now trim your airplane for about a hundred miles an hour, so it will kind of glide hands off. Your prop ought to be turning around twenty-two hundred, twenty-four hundred rpm. Why don't you set about ten inches of manifold pressure? Just throttle it back until it settles to about a hundred miles an hour. Still see me?

XYZ: This is XYZ. I have got it trimmed to a hundred miles an hour, and I'm losing you.

PIPER: All right, we are just on the tops of the clouds. Now you just stay one four zero about a hundred miles an hour, and about ten inches of manifold pressure on your throttle.

XYZ: This is XYZ. I have lost you again.

PIPER: The clouds are getting a little too thick. Can't fly formation quite close enough, but you are heading south of Red Bluff right now. You are in fine shape as long as you can make your compass read right around one four, one four on the compass, just so your airplane is going downhill. Around a hundred miles an hour.

XYZ: XYZ, I'm at thirty-five hundred feet, ninety miles an hour.

PIPER: That's good, you're doing real good, just keep her coming on down. I'm at three thousand, so I'm lower than you are.

XYZ: This is XYZ.

PIPER: Okay, XYZ, seven five, a hundred miles an hour or thereabouts. Try ten inches of manifold pressure. Try to keep that little old needle in that turn and bank indicator pointing straight up in the center. You work the rudder pedals to work that little needle.

XYZ: I'm at three thousand feet now. I can't see nothing.

PIPER: That's okay. I'm at twenty-five, and as long as you stay on one four on the compass at a hundred miles an hour and the needle centered—why, you got it made.

XYZ: I can't hold it on one four for some reason. I'm at three thousand feet. I'm on— Hell! I'm on three degrees.

PIPER: Okay, just push on the right rudder now a little bit and make the needle swing to the right on the gauge, so when your compass reads about one four again, you'll be out and you'll be able to see the ground at two thousand feet. I can see the ground now. I'm at two thousand feet. I can see the lights, and we're in real good shape here, so I'll wait down here for you.

XYZ: I'm having trouble holding it on a heading.

PIPER: Let it go down a little faster.

XYZ: I got it on a heading now of twenty-four degrees.

PIPER: Okay, push on the left rudder pedal a little bit there. You probably want to turn to the left.

XYZ: Six hundred feet now.

PIPER: What's your altitude?

XYZ: Hundred miles an hour.

OAKLAND: Seven five pop, can you get him down through it a little faster?

PIPER: Okay, we're going to hurry it up. XYZ, seven five. What's your altitude?

XYZ: This is XYZ. I'm at twenty-five hundred feet at about ninety miles an hour, I've got no idea of what the hell heading I have.

PIPER: Okay, just close your throttle all the way. Close your throttle all the way. You're bound to come out within a few miles of the airport. Do you know where your carburetor heat is? Pull it on to just play safe.

XYZ: XYZ, I am at about two thousand feet.

PIPER: All right. Do you see the airport at Red Bluff? Are you sure you're over Red Bluff?

XYZ: Yes I do!

PIPER: Okay, go ahead and land then. Seven five will cancel IFR with the center.

XYZ: This is XYZ. What direction am I supposed to land here?

PIPER: I would say it wouldn't make much difference tonight. Just pick a runway out and land on it. I'll call and tell them you're coming in.

OAKLAND: Seven five pop, Red Bluff radio has him in sight now.

PIPER: Okay. Well, I guess he got away with it then. Thank you.

OAKLAND: Thank you very much.

PIPER: Righto.

OAKLAND: Can you see him landing?

PIPER: I think I did. I'm not sure.

XYZ: This is XYZ. I'm having trouble with my landing gear now!

PIPER: Okay, just pull back on it, and just give it a good hard yank.

XYZ: I am going to land to the north.

PIPER: Did you get your wheels down?

XYZ: Got the wheels down.

PIPER: Oakland, we got him in sight. I guess we're going to have to tie up until we actually see him on the ground though.

OAKLAND: Seven five pop, that's fine. Red Bluff has him in sight also now. Coming in landing to the north.

PIPER: He's on the downwind leg.

OAKLAND: Seven five pop, can you tell him to turn on his landing lights? . . . Seven five pop, he's got his landing lights on.

PIPER: Okay. He's on the ground, safe and sound.

Appendix B

Administrators of the Federal Aviation Administration and Its Predecessor Agencies

---

AERONAUTICS BRANCH, DEPARTMENT OF COMMERCE

Assistant Secretary of Commerce for Aeronautics:
William P.

MacCracken, Jr.	August 11, 1926–October 1, 1929
Clarence M. Young	October 1, 1929–March 4, 1933

Director of Aeronautics:

Eugene L. Vidal	October 1, 1933–June 30, 1934

BUREAU OF AIR COMMERCE, DEPARTMENT OF COMMERCE

Director of Air Commerce:

Eugene L. Vidal	July 1, 1934–March 1, 1937
Fred D. Fagg, Jr.	March 1, 1937–April 15, 1938
Denis Mulligan	April 16, 1938–August 8, 1938

CIVIL AERONAUTICS AUTHORITY

Chairman:

Edward J. Noble	August 22, 1938–April 12, 1939
Robert H. Hinckley	April 12, 1939–July 8, 1940

Administrator:

Clinton M. Hester   August 22, 1938–June 30, 1940

CIVIL AERONAUTICS ADMINISTRATION

Administrator:

Donald H. Connolly	July 11, 1940–January 15, 1942
Charles I. Stanton	May 27, 1942–August 22, 1944
Theodore P. Wright	August 22, 1944–January 14, 1948
Delos W. Rentzel	April 8, 1948–September 18, 1950
Donald W. Nyrop	September 19, 1950–March 18, 1951
Charles F. Horne	March 19, 1951–March 6, 1953
Frederick B. Lee	March 11, 1953–December 8, 1955
Charles J. Lowen	December 12, 1955–September 5, 1956
James T. Pyle	December 20, 1956–December 30, 1958

FEDERAL AVIATION ADMINISTRATION

Administrator:

Elwood R. Quesada	November 1, 1958–January 20, 1961
Najeeb E. Halaby	January 20, 1961–June 30, 1965
William F. McKee	June 30, 1965–

Appendix C

Summary of FAA Budget Estimates Fiscal Year 1968

| Appropriation | New Obligational Authority | | |
	1967 [a]	1968	Difference [b]
Operations	$577,169,000	$598,400,000	$21,231,000
Facilities and equipment	28,000,000	35,400,000	7,400,000
Research and development	28,500,000	27,500,000	−1,000,000
Operation and maintenance, national capital airports	8,527,000	8,500,000	−27,000
Construction, national capital airports	—	160,000	160,000
Grants-in-aid for airports	71,000,000	71,000,000	—
Subtotal	713,196,000	740,960,000	+27,764,000
Civil supersonic aircraft development	280,000,000	—	−280,000,000
Total, new obligational authority	$993,196,000	$740,960,000	$−252,236,000

[a] Includes supplemental appropriations of $18,895,000 for pay increase costs proposed for separate transmittal to the Congress.

[b] The negative difference is accounted for by the fact that 1968 funding for the civil supersonic aircraft development program is not included. For agency activities other than the SST program, the estimated 1968 budget provides for an incease of $27.8 million.

SOURCE: FAA background information briefing, January 24, 1967.

Appendix D
Letter to Mr. Halaby (See Chapter III)

FEDERAL AVIATION AGENCY
EASTERN REGION
Federal Building
NEW YORK INTERNATIONAL AIRPORT
Jamaica, New York

December 18, 1961

Mr. N. E. Halaby
1711 New York Avenue
Washington 25, D.C.

Dear Mr. Halaby:

This office has received a report disclosing that on
November 9, 1961, you, the holder of Commercial Pilot
Certificate No. 69841-41, while piloting public aircraft
bearing identification No. N-1 [Gulfstream] on takeoff
from Runway 15, at Washington National Airport, neglected
to provide adequate clearance from a United Air Lines'
Viscount standing in the run-up area for Runway 15,
awaiting takeoff clearance and that you permitted the left
wing tip of N-1 to contact the ring wing tip of the
Viscount, thus causing damage to both wing tips. The
foregoing indicates that you failed to exercise the care
and caution required of the holder of a pilot certificate and consequently, that your operation was contrary
to section 60.12 of the Civil Air Regulations and Section
610(a) of the Federal Aviation Act of 1958 (72 Stat.
780).

By reason of the above violation, pursuant to Section 901
of the said Act, you are subject to a civil penalty of
not to exceed $1000.00. This office is authorized to
accept a lesser amount in compromise of such penalty. In
accordance with usual procedures, we have evaluated the
incident to determine what sanction, if any, should be
imposed. We note that you have acknowledged full respon-

sibility: that safety of flight operations was not compromised and that in your previous twenty-eight years of flying, you have not been involved in any accident or cited for violation of safety regulations.

Upon full consideration of the foregoing, we have determined that an offer of $50.00 in full settlement of the civil penalty incurred would be acceptable. Enclosed is an explanation of the compromise process.

Sincerely yours,

MARTIN J. WHITE
Regional Counsel

Enclosure

EA-240, CC-30, FS-870, PA-1

Appendix E

Location of FAA Regional and Area Offices

Area Office

CENTRAL REGION

Chicago — 3166 Des Plaines Avenue, Des Plaines, Ill. 60018
Kansas City* — 4747 Troost Avenue, Kansas City, Mo. 64110
Minneapolis — 6301 34th Avenue, South Minneapolis, Minn. 55450

EASTERN REGION

Boston — N.W. Industrial Park, Burlington, Mass. 01804
Cleveland — 21010 Center Ridge Road, Rocky River, Ohio 44116
New York* — JFK International Airport, Jamaica, N.Y. 11430
Washington — 800 Independence Avenue, S.W., Washington, D.C. 20553

SOUTHERN REGION

Atlanta* — 3400 Whipple Street, East Point, Ga. 30320
Memphis — 3400 Democrat Road, Memphis, Tenn. 38118
Miami — International Airport, Miami, Fla. 33159

SOUTHWESTERN REGION

Albuquerque — East Central and San Mateo streets, Albuquerque, N.M. 87108

Fort Worth*   Building #4, Haslet Road, Fort Worth,
                   Tex. 76101
Houston   8345 Telephone Road, Houston, Tex. 77060

WESTERN REGION

Denver   8055 East 32nd Avenue, Denver, Colo. 80207
Los Angeles*   5885 West Imperial Highway, Los Angeles,
                   Calif. 90045
Salt Lake City   116 North 23rd West, Salt Lake City,
                   Utah 84116
San Francisco   831 Mitten Road, Burlingame, California 94010
Seattle   Boeing Field, Seattle, Wash. 98108

*FAA regional headquarters located at the same address.

Appendix F

FAA Promotion and Recruitment Policies

The FAA staff numbers approximately 44,000 workers, most of whom are highly trained specialists in some phase of aeronautics or air traffic control. The average FAA employee has a civil service grade level of GS-10 and in 1966 earned an average salary of $10,600 a year. A little more than one-third of all FAA employees are employed in air traffic control activities. Approximately 20 per cent are electronic technicians, and their numbers are growing as the agency continues to automate not only its air traffic control work but many of its routine activities.

As might be expected from an organization employing so many highly skilled workers, the turnover rate of FAA employees is among the lowest for any government agency. During 1965, for example, the separation rate was 7.2 employees per year per 100 positions. In the same year, the government average was 19.2. Separation rate for FAA air traffic controllers was only 2.48, well below the agency's over-all average. A further indication of the high morale enjoyed by FAA employees is the fact that they rank among the most conservative users of sick leave in the federal government. The average FAA employee has consistently used only slightly more than one-half of the 104 hours he earns for this purpose each year.

Why are FAA employees so work-oriented? One reason is that agency employees as a group are well-paid professionals who take pride in their jobs and in the important role they play in the business of aviation. Another is that, when filling job vacancies, FAA is well aware of the advantages of promoting from within the agency,

243

a practice which opens up a chain of employee opportunities. Some ways used by FAA to make vacancies available to its own personnel are: (1) job engineering—writing jobs to take advantage of available qualifications; (2) training agreements—to assist promising employees to qualify for jobs when candidates fully meeting qualification requirements are not available; and (3) developmental reassignments.

Career planning is a vital force in FAA's personnel system. It identifies future manpower needs and ties them into current training programs; it cultivates existing skills, sets career patterns, and develops required new skills.

Although aviation activity is expected to continue to increase over the next several years, FAA employment is expected to remain relatively stable, declining somewhat over the next several years as employees and management work together to bring about improvements in productivity. These improvements are dependent upon the introduction of manpower-saving equipment, particularly in en route traffic control facilities and flight inspection programs, as well as continued advances in work scheduling and other managament techniques.

Because of this improved utilization of manpower, the large-scale recruitment and training efforts expended by FAA during its formative years have given way to more sophisticated, "individually tailored" programs responsive to the present needs of the agency. Recruitment and training programs, which formerly were directed at hiring and training large numbers of basically qualified air traffic controllers and electronic maintenance technicians, now emphasize individual quality and selectivity in hiring and promoting, as well as upgrading of individual skills, career development, and management training.

Nearly all FAA jobs come under the civil service merit system. Job selections are made on the basis of ability to do the work. The Civil Service Commission issues announcements for examinations for specific types of positions when there is a need to fill such positions. Current job announcements are available at most post offices and all regional and Washington civil service offices. FAA Washington headquarters, regional, and area personnel offices (see addresses in Appendix E) have current information on FAA job openings within their geographical jurisdictions.

Bibliography

The best source of information about the Federal Aviation Administration, its history, and that of its predecessor agencies is the agency itself. More than fifty publications are available from the FAA. These range from small illustrated pamphlets—such as "Flight U.S.A.," which describes a typical commercial airline flight from New York City to Washington, D.C., as seen by the air traffic control specialists—to the massive nine-volume research report on the supersonic transport released in April, 1967. Of the many FAA publications available, only those that were of particular help to the author in preparing this volume are included below. Readers having need of additional official reference material may want to write the FAA (800 Independence Avenue S.W., Washington, D.C. 20950) and ask either for the twenty-two-page booklet that lists FAA publications, available free for sale, or for the FAA Aviation Education Division's enlarged bibliography of reference materials, including FAA films.

"About Sabotage," *The Air Line Pilot*, Vol. 35. Chicago: Air Line Pilots Association (October, 1966) pp. 12–14.

Accelerated Modernization of the U.S. Air Traffic Control and Navigation System. Prepared by the Air Coordinating Committee. Washington, D.C.: Office of Technical Services, U.S. Department of Commerce, 1957.

Airlines. Report of the Antitrust Subcommittee of the Committee on the Judiciary of the House of Representatives, 85th Cong. 1st Sess. Washington, D.C.: U.S. Government Printing Office, 1957.

Career Opportunities with the Airlines. Washington, D.C.: Air Transport Association, 1967.

CHERRINGTON, PAUL. *Status and Economic Significance of the Airline Equipment Investment Program.* Washington, D.C.: The White House, 1958.

CURTIS, EDWARD P. *National Requirements for Aviation Facilities: 1956–75.* Washington, D.C.: U.S. Government Printing Office, 1957.

Federal Aviation Agency. *Annual Reports* (for the years 1959–66). Washington, D.C.: U.S. Government Printing Office.

The Federal Aviation Agency. Washington, D.C.: U.S. Government Printing Office, 1964.

FAA Statistical Handbook of Aviation. Washington, D.C.: U.S. Government Printing Office, 1966. Published annually.

"FAA Studies Crash-Test Data . . . ," *FAA/Aviation News*, Vol. 3. Washington, D.C.: Federal Aviation Agency (June, 1964) p. 35.

GLASS, FRED M. *Report of the Task Force on National Aviation Goals.* Washington, D.C.: U.S. Government Printing Office, 1961.

HALABY, N. E. *Policy Statement of the Federal Aviation Agency.* Washington, D.C.: Federal Aviation Agency, 1965.

————. *Statement of U.S. International Air Transport Policy.* Washington, D.C.: The White House, 1963.

KIMBALL, DAN A. *Report of the Aviation Human Resources Study Board On Manpower Requirements of the Civil Aviation Industry.* Washington, D.C.: U.S. Government Printing Office, 1964.

MOHLER, STANLEY R. *Recent Findings on the Impairment of Airmanship by Alcohol.* Washington, D.C.: Federal Aviation Agency, 1966.

REDFORD, EMMETTE S. *Congress Passes the Federal Aviation Act of 1958.* University, Ala.: University of Alabama Press, 1961.

RHYNE, CHARLES S. *The Civil Aeronautics Act Annotated.* Washington, D.C.: National Law Book Company, 1939.

SERLING, ROBERT J. *The Electra Story.* New York: Doubleday & Co., 1963.

————. *The Probable Cause.* New York: Ballantine Books, 1964.

"Washington and Workload," *The Flight Service Journal,* Vol. 8. Bethesda, Md.: National Association of Air Traffic Specialists (September, 1966), pp. 4–6.

WHITNAH, DONALD R. *Safer Skyways.* Ames, Iowa: Iowa State University Press, 1967. This scholarly work is particularly valuable for its historical research on the origins of federal control over civil aviation and for its extensive bibliography of publications and other reference material available.

Index